Reinvent Your Happiness

Five Steps to Your Best Self in 2017

Chuck Bolton
Bestselling Author

The Reinvention Imperative Publishing

Notice

Copyright ©Chuck Bolton
All Rights reserved

This book is dedicated to Mary who brings me such great happiness. You inspire me every day to be my best.

Reinvent Your Happiness: Five Steps to Your Best Self in 2017

Table of Contents

The Game of Catch

When I was 8 years old, I was a happy 3rd grader, without a care in the world, living in a small town in Kentucky with my parents, Helen and Jack Bolton.

The daughter of Swedish immigrants, Helen had wanted to be a missionary when she was young; she knew how to love and take care of people. Jack was a manager at a factory. At 6'4", 250 pounds, he was like a mountain, in my eyes: My hero.

Every day, my Dad and I played a game of catch. And throwing the baseball with dad, every night, was my favorite thing. Every night, after he returned home from the plant, he heard me ask: "Daddy, daddy! Can we play catch?"

One Sunday morning in late August will forever be burned in my memory. I awoke to an empty house. A few hours later, Mom, tears streaming down her face walked in the front door. She said she had taken dad to the emergency room. She sobbed, and uttered two haunting words: "Daddy died."

We'd played catch just the night before. Now he was gone – forever – felled by a massive heart attack. My happiness vanished. I no longer took interest in school, friends--or really, much of anything. Because the game of catch was over.

That winter, Mom took matters in her own hands. She saved the S&H Green Stamps they gave you at the Winn-Dixie supermarket when you bought groceries. One warm Saturday morning in March--early spring in Kentucky--Mom said we needed to go to Louisville to run errands. She drove us to the S&H store. She told the man behind the counter that she wanted to get the catcher's mitt that appeared on page 34 of their catalog.

More than seven months had passed since I'd last played catch. Dad and I were both left-handed, but Mom was a righty; she couldn't use his old first baseman's mitt.

Mom handed over the stamp books, and took the mitt, and we went on our way. The game of catch was about to resume.

Even though Mom wasn't that great at catch, she gave it her best. We played for three years – until I was 11. We filled the holes in our hearts that way. Slowly, the happiness returned.

Shortly before my 12th birthday, Mom and I moved to Chicago. To support us, she needed to begin working as a secretary-- and to care for her parents, who were in failing health. She told me I could ride my bike to the park to play Little League baseball. There, as she had predicted, I found plenty of other boys to play catch. She retired the catcher's mitt—but by then, it had served its purpose.

That game of catch with Mom was a great gift. She got me over the hump of losing Dad that way. She got me playing organized baseball, and pitching. That was an activity I could throw myself into – I was happy being on the team and playing ball. Pitching ultimately helped pay for my college education. I was blessed to play college ball, under the tutelage of outstanding coaches. I also had caring professors, and a great four years in school.

Without that game of catch with mom, I wouldn't have...

- Gone to college.

- Enjoyed a 20-year career as a leader in the fast-growing medical device industry.

- Become a CEO coach, coached a Nobel Prize-winner, written a best selling book, or given a speech at the Harvard Business School.

Nor would I be showing leaders and teams how to reinvent themselves and become happier -- so they can discover how to become their best and become even more successful.

Mom was a happy leader. A great role model. She was the person who was most generous, optimistic and inspiring. She taught me to care about others. For her, what seemed to be huge problems were challenges to be chunked down and conquered. From her, I learned how to treat people, how to handle life's curveballs, and when to swing for the fences -- lessons I use daily in my work.

She had to reinvent herself, from homemaker to single parent, breadwinner, and caregiver. She never complained; she always smiled, and encouraged others with her happiness. Mom was the most remarkable person I've ever met.

And, Mom told me always to give my best—and become my best. She was my role model for happiness and reinvention. This book is for her. And for you. To help you become happier, more successful, to become your best.

It's time to get started.

2016 is Over!

I t's the afternoon of December 29, 2016. Taking it easy this afternoon at home. In a few hours, Mary and I will drive to St. Paul to watch our favorite National Hockey League team, the Minnesota Wild, play the New York Islanders and compete for their 12th straight win - a franchise record. Thinking about the hours ahead, what a fun evening lies in store for us.

Anticipating enjoyable events is a double banger in the happiness department. With the game scheduled on the calendar, you get to look forward to the function, and when it's time, you get to enjoy it. Add that I'll share the evening with my beautiful partner and maybe it becomes a triple banger for happiness! I can't wait for tonight.

But prior to the evening ahead, I'm relaxing in my favorite chair, enjoying a roaring fire on an overcast, 30 degree Minnesota winter day, reflecting on the year 2016. In a few short days, the new year greets us.

Reading my gratitude journal entries and reflecting back to the days, weeks and months of 2016, on a personal level, I feel blessed to recall many wonderful memories with family and friends. It's been a year of good health and abundance. My work is purposeful and business has been strong. Overall, it's been a happy year.

But as I reflect on the year from a broader, more global perspective, what a year it has been! Does it feel like 2016 has torn us apart? Sure, there have been some heartwarming moments we've experienced; but a lot of misery has also transpired this year. It's been a challenging year. Here are a few of the 2016 takeaways:

- We've seen a contentious and divisive election in the USA, that has as a new president preparing to take office on January 20;

- We've seen an era end in Cuba with the death of Fidel Castro;

- We've seen Haiti's worst humanitarian crisis this decade with Hurricane Matthew.

- We've seen continued tension and violence between police and communities;

- We've seen terrorism in Florida, France, Turkey, Belgium and Germany;

- We've learned to be terrified of the Zika virus;

- We've seen the United Kingdom pass the "Brexit" referendum, signaling Britain's withdrawal from the European Union;

- We've seen the horrors of Aleppo and the continued suffering of the Syrian people;

- We've seen Russia behaving badly;

- We've lost many in the public eye. David Bowie, Nancy Reagan, Merle Haggard, Antonin Scalia, Janet Reno, Muhammad Ali, Arnold Palmer, Gordie Howe, Craig Sager, Leonard Cohen, Prince and George Michael. Two days ago, we lost Carrie Fisher, and, yesterday, her mother Debbie Reynolds;

On a happier note:

- We've seen another Olympics come and go.

- We've seen a 108-year losing streak end with the Chicago Cubs winning the World Series (Sorry, Cleveland Indians fans, you had your fun in June with the Cavaliers winning the NBA Championship, ending a 65-year championship drought for your city!);

- We've watched the US unemployment rate sink to 4.6%, the lowest in 10 years;

- All those annoying campaign ads are a thing of the past!

The year is over, becoming yet another "Auld Lang Syne". Let's hope 2017 will be as good as 2016 was challenging.

Let's also decide to control what we can. No matter the circumstances. We can choose happiness. Read along with me, do the "happiness work" and I'll show you how to raise your happiness! Let's agree to do our part to stack the deck for a happy 2017.

What's Happened to Happiness?

"Happiness is the whole aim of human existence."
— Aristotle

Happiness.

Everyone wants it. We've chased it since the beginning of time. Some people won't openly say they wish to be happy, but they, too, desire happiness – however they describe it. After all, who gets up in the morning saying, "I hope this will be a rotten day. I hope I'll be unhappy"?

There's a universal desire for a good, happy life; but most people aren't satisfied with their lives. Few are truly happy.

This is a big problem. Because when you're not happy, it's impossible to be as creative, productive and successful as you could be. Yet it doesn't have to be that way.

Too many are too busy, too distracted, living unhealthy, "linear" lives – burning the candle at both ends. They are surrounded by, and accept, mediocrity. Your happiness with the key parts of life: relationships, health and fitness, faith, career, money, fun – probably falls short of your expectations. When you are unable to or unsuccessful in making positive changes in your life, you become unhappy, and fail to thrive. You languish.

Why is Happiness so Important?

Why is happiness so important? Because it brings you well-being. It makes you optimistic and enthusiastic. It drives success, as well as good health and solid relationships. Happiness is serious business.

Happiness Drives Success

Greg Jacobson's ***Think Yourself Happy: Five Changes in Thinking that Will Immediately Improve Your Lif****e*, says, "People who are happy: Are more productive. Live longer. Have improved health. Have stronger, longer-lasting relationships. Are married longer and have lower divorce rates. Report greater life satisfaction. Earn more money. Have a more positive attitude. Contribute more. Learn faster and easier. Are more enjoyable to be around. Are better team players. Make fewer mistakes. Are more creative. Are better problem-solvers and solve problems faster." [1]

Research has shown that happiness offers many rewards. When you intentionally work on becoming happier, you feel better, boost your energy and creativity, become more productive and live longer.

In ***The Happiness Advantage: The 7 Principles of Positive Psychology that Fuel Success and Performance at Work***, Shawn Achor writes that happiness is more than a good feeling – it is an indispensable component of our success. It precedes success.

But often happiness seems elusive in today's crazy busy world. As a matter of fact, it seems to be on the decline. It shouldn't be that way.

---

[1] Jacobson, Greg. *Think Yourself Happy: Five Changes in Thinking that Will Immediately Improve Your Life*

The State of Happiness is Low

Here's a HUGE problem: Most of us aren't happy. Research shows low levels of happiness among adults in the US.

For example, only 45% of us are happy in our jobs, reported *The Conference Board* survey in 2010: the lowest percentage in 22 years of polling.

The rate of depression today is 10 times higher than in 1960. Each year the threshold of unhappiness sinks across the nation, at work, school and home.[2]

According to Joseph McClendon III in his book, *Get Happy Now!*, only an estimated 3.5% of people are happy, positive and optimistic. [3]

Dan Baker and Cameron Stauth, in *What Happy People Know: The New Science of Happiness Can Change Your Life for the Better,* report "...approximately 2/3s of

---

[2] Shawn Achor. *The Happiness Advantage: The 7 Principles of Positive Psychology that Fuel Success and Performance at Work*
[3] Joseph McClendon III. *Get Happy Now!*

American subjects in a recent study describe themselves as 'not very happy.'"[4]

As the world become more connected and the desire to flourish increases, everyone everywhere wants to live a happy life.

The small Himalayan country, Bhutan, has made happiness a national priority. Bhutan has a Gross National Happiness measurement. They are addressing the important question for their people: "What makes for better lives?"

The United Arab Emirates (UAE) named its first ever minister of state for happiness, Ohood Al Roumi, on February 10, 2016. Her appointment was announced by Sheikh Mohammed. He tweeted, "She will align and drive government policy to create social good and satisfaction. The National Agenda aims for the UAE to be among the best in the world in the Human Development Index and to be the happiest of all nations so that its citizens feel proud to belong to the UAE."

The **World Happiness Report 2016** is a measure of happiness published by the United Nations, following the UN's 2011 resolution inviting member countries to measure the happiness of their people and use this information to help guide public policies. It identities six key factors: GDP per capita, life expectancy, social support, trust, generosity and perceived freedom to make life decisions.

In 2016, the US was 13th of 158 countries in happiness.[5]

---

[4] Dan Baker and Cameron Stauth. *What Happy People Know: How the New Science of Happiness Can Change Your Life for the Better*

[5] Sustainable Development Solutions Network. *World Happiness Report 2016*

The top 20 happiest countries were:

1. Denmark

2. Switzerland

3. Iceland

4. Norway

5. Finland

6. Canada

7. The Netherlands

8. New Zealand

9. Australia

10. Sweden

11. Israel

12. Austria

13. USA

14. Costa Rica

15. Puerto Rico

16. Germany

17. Brazil

18. Belgium

19. Ireland

20. Luxembourg

This past year, nearly 1500 people took **The Happiness Report** survey at TheHappinessReport.com. Both women and men, ages 20 - 80, were asked to rate their happiness, on a scale of 1 to 10, statements that corresponded to the eight most important parts of life: Fun, Career, Spiritual Fulfillment, Health and Fitness, Finances, Significant Other, Family, and Friends. Each respondent received **The Happiness Report,** with his or her overall score (1 to 100) and score in each of the eight parts.[6]

On a scale of 1 to 10, _the average score was 6.9._ Put another way, that's **69%.**

Think back to your school days: 69 was a letter D grade. A D is a 1.0 GPA. Below average. Mediocre. Unacceptable.

---

[6] Chuck Bolton. *The State of Our Happiness in 2017: What We've Discovered*

Yet we're scoring a "D" in the happiness of our lives!

Here's the breakdown by gender and by category, highest to lowest. Men are slightly more happy than women.

Average Scores – The Happiness Report

Women		Men	
Dimension	*Avg Score*	*Dimension*	*Avg Score*
1. Family	78	1. Family	76
2. Friends	73	2. Fun	75
3. Fun	72	3. Career	72
4. Career	69	4. Financial	70
5. Spiritual	67	5. Friends	69
6. Financial	63	6. Significant Other	69
7. Significant Other	63	7. Spiritual	67
8. Health & Fitness	62	8. Health & Fitness	67
OVERALL	**69**	**OVERALL**	**71**

The satisfaction of females was highest in the family and friends parts, lowest in health & fitness and significant others.

For males, family and fun ranked highest, while health and fitness and spiritual were rated lowest.

Thirty-five percent of the survey takers were in the GenX generation. Millennials comprised thirty percent of the survey population while Baby Boomers made up twenty-four percent. Millennials scored happiest, followed by Baby Boomers with the GenX generation coming in last.

The State of Our Happiness as a country is mediocre. We have a long way to go to be happier and thrive.

For more information on the cumulative results from *The Happiness Report*, go to Appendix A and see the presentation: *The State of Our Happiness in 2017: What We've Discovered*.

Back to your happiness? How happy are you in the eight key areas of life? Go to TheHappinessReport.com to take your free assessment and receive your feedback results.

Given our desire for happy, healthy and abundant lives –- why do we settle for emotional mediocrity? And more important, what can we do about it? It's your birthright to be happy. You must never give it up. If you have ever given your happiness to anyone or anything, you must reclaim it.

Here's good news: You can reinvent how you think and behave, and increase your happiness, if you know how. In the past decade, findings in the field of neuroscience prove this. This book will show you how, and how to sustain happiness, so you can flourish.

Our method isn't drawing smiley faces. It consists of proven techniques. It may be the most important book you'll read. Apply these techniques, and you'll become happier. And that is good not only for you, but for everyone you come in contact with, at home and work. After all, happiness is contagious.

Making this happen begins with your logbook. Like a ship captain, you track your journey. After all, you are the captain of your life.

Keep a Logbook

Writing, drawing, you enter the story of your reinvention into it. I recommend the 8.5" x 11" Blick sketchbook.

http://www.dickblick.com/products/blick-hardbound-sketchbook/

Why a logbook? What's wrong with a tablet or laptop? Writing in longhand is important. Holding and moving the pen sends feedback signals to the brain, creating "motor memory." It stimulates synapses between left and right hemispheres, absent in typing, that make you more creative and thoughtful.

Sit in a comfortable chair. Turn on some relaxing music, if you like--and get busy.

As you get started, reflect and answer the following:

How Happy are You?

Right now, today, on a scale of 1 to 10, how happy are you?

Write it down. Done? Good!

Now, on a scale of 1 to 10, how happy would you like to be?

Write it down. I hope you seek at least 9, if not 10!

All right, let's get started.

The Crazy Busy World

What is going on these days? One thing is for sure, things ain't the way they used to be. They gets crazier and busier all the time, it seems.

First, the craziness. What's the usual response you hear when you ask someone how he's doing? "I'm OK."

If you reply, "OK, how are you REALLY doing?" you'll usually hear, "I'm busy!" Sometimes, "I'm crazy busy!"

That has often been my answer to the question. And, to tell the truth, it isn't so much a complaint, but a merit badge I gladly display, because if I can persuade you I'm busy, then I must surely be important. Doesn't matter if I'm busy doing the right things. You've got to a respect an important, busy person. You can't get upset at a busy guy, can you?

Deep down, I feel if I'm not busy, I'm a slacker. The reality of that "busyness" is, I'm the one in the driver's seat. The hurry and busyness is generally self-imposed. And this busyness becomes an addiction.

I feel like I'm slacking if I'm not doing something related to work, that helps build my business, or serve a client. So when I watch a movie with my family in our family room, sending a few emails from my somewhat inconspicuous iPad seems OK.

I'm hurried, unable to be fully present. (If you don't believe this, just ask Mary or my kids!)

We justify our busyness by an insidious dialogue we have with ourselves. "It's harder than ever to be successful. Therefore, I'd better be busy, and not take my eye off the ball, or bad things will happen."

A recent study showed people use their smartphones on average five hours a day, check it 85 times a day. And we wonder why we suffer self-imposed "techno-stress." Busy to the max! We distract ourselves, rapidly toggling between tasks: multi-tasking. Unable to concentrate on one thing, we feel overwhelmed.

We pile on work, then outside activities, as we're addicted to busyness--exhausted, yet fearing what we might do without a frenetic schedule. We hurry, unable to be present for even a few moments. This malady has a name: hurry sickness. We load up stress and anxiety when we are overly busy, and burn the candle at both ends.

Sadly, it is not just adults. We've loaded up the kids with sports and extracurricular activities, classes and homework assignments. They feel as wiped out as we do.

Does busyness increase happiness? The answer is a resounding **no.** A study from Stanford University showed "...those who spend considerable amounts of time using multimedia describe themselves in ways that suggest they are less happy and less socially comfortable than peers who say they spend less time on screens."

This busyness raises a fair question. "Are you too busy to be happy?"

Does this sound familiar? If so, you aren't alone.

When I speak to groups of busy executives, I'll often ask, "If you are busier today than you were two years ago, raise your hand?" Without fail, every hand goes up.

"Do you anticipate being busier next year than you've been this year?" Moving in chairs, shifting of eyes, and slowly, the hands start going up. "How is that going to work?" Grumbling.

Perhaps when I feel more on top of the world, when I feel a bit more in control and experiencing some success, I'll allow myself to feel happy. Does that really work? No! Because happiness drives success--not the other way around.

The truth is, you're each a bundle of habits. You pick them up, without questioning them, practice them for years and years. You stick to your habits, even if they aren't in your best interest. You become a Repeater.

Some habits are good, like brushing your teeth after each meal. To experience greater happiness, you'll need to develop some more positive habits, and drop bad ones. This sets you up for positive feelings and happiness. Carefully rethink how you invest your energy and time, so you don't live a linear life, and burn out. You don't have to be so busy that you can't be happy.

When you are too busy and distracted, you languish and suffer. When you accept mediocrity, others languish and suffer, too.

You can experience anxiety, loneliness, loss of self-esteem, eating and sleeping problems, unhappiness, depression, and substance abuse. This may cause you to fail to become the person you wanted to be, meet your potential, to live a Purposeful Life, the life you envisioned. When you aren't happy, your family and those you love suffer, too. They aren't getting the best "you."

To increase your happiness, not to mention your ability to make a sustained contribution, break the busyness trap, by using your mind. That's how you become more happy and more successful.

In this book, you'll discover a five-step framework, proven, easy to understand and apply, to increase your happiness, and put you on the path to thrive and flourish: living with happiness, purpose, and intention.

Can You Really Change Your Worry to Happiness?

Can you change worry to happiness? And can you make positive change stick? The short answer is an emphatic, "Yes and yes!"

Many of you worry yourselves into anxiety and unhappiness.

"Worrying does not empty tomorrow of its troubles it empties today of its strength."
— Corrie Ten Boom

Maggie, a friend of mine, is an experienced music teacher who switched schools earlier this year. She replaced a well-liked teacher, Annie, who relocated to another state.

In her first semester, the other teachers, and some students who remembered Annie's routine and habits, reminded her how Annie did things. Annie had a larger-than-life reputation with staff, parents and students. And replacing her was a tall order for Maggie.

Held the second week in December, the Holiday Concert, combining the 4th through 6th grades, was Maggie's opportunity to prove to the other teachers, staff, and parents that she could pull off a successful production. As November turned to December, Maggie became increasingly worried about the concert. She was a nervous wreck. She felt the students weren't practicing the songs at home, and, as the last few rehearsals took place, she was worried too many had failed to memorize the lyrics--that the concert would be an abysmal failure. The week before the concert, she couldn't sleep; run down, she fretted herself into a bad cold. She dwelled on the worst possible outcome, how embarrassing and damaging it would be for her, and feared she'd continue to be overshadowed by Annie. She obsessed that her principal and other teachers wouldn't feel she was a good music teacher. She worried about disappointing the parents, grandparents, and other family members and friends in the audience of 500.

The weekend before her Tuesday concert, Maggie reached out to me. In listening to her, it was clear that she'd prepared her charges well. She'd done all that she could; "the hay was in the barn." We discussed that when it was show time Tuesday night, the students would likely be concentrating intently, excited to perform. Rehearsals were one thing – performances were another. We talked about how it was unlikely going to be perfect, but perfection is never attainable, anyway. Despite flaws, the families would be excited to see their kids perform.

As she'd done everything she could to ensure a successful performance, a more effective strategy would be to visualize the best performance possible, have faith the students would deliver, and enjoy herself. As Maggie let those words sink in, she smiled a big smile. You could see the weight lifted off her shoulders. Optimism would serve her well.

After our talk, she reminded herself of all the reasons why the performance would be a success. She said any hints of worry caused her to pause, recalling that that was her ego playing tricks on her.

Later that week, Maggie called me to report the concert had gone fabulously well; her students enjoyed themselves, and the adoration they received from their families. Maggie received many compliments from parents, her principal and co-workers. Maggie was happy, back to herself, and determined not to let worry creep in for future concerts.

Worrying is not what makes the happiest and most successful people get ahead. They use their brains and vision to succeed. Their brains drive their happiness, and the success flows.

However, what dominates your thinking governs how you live your life. So whatever you concentrate on, you'll get corresponding results. It's your choice: dwell on the negative, receive negative outcomes. Or emphasize the positive, and succeed.

Neuroscience has shown the brain is malleable, not static. It possesses neuroplasticity, which means it can change throughout your life. Studies have shown many ways you can "rewire" your brain to be more positive, resilient and creative. Your thoughts, daily activities, and behaviors drive the changes in your brain. That includes lasting positive change, leading to greater happiness.

Knowing the brain can change, however, is insufficient. To reinvent ourselves, to change our behavior and create lasting change and happiness, takes intentional concentration, effort to put the principles into effect. Once you do, you'll be happier. You need the will to change, and some skills.

What's Required to Reinvent

Skill

Will

The Components of Happiness

As you seek to become happier, *50/10/40* is an important combination to remember.

Fifty percent of your happiness is your "set range." In other words, half of your happiness is determined by genetics: it can be attributed to your parents. This baseline for happiness is one that you'll gravitate towards naturally, even after you've experienced great accomplishments or spectacular failures. [7]

But your circumstances account for only 10% of your happiness! Think about people who've suffered mightily: death of a loved one, loss of a job, career setback, an unsatisfying or abusive relationship, a financial disaster, or a catastrophic event like a tornado or earthquake that wiped out home and possessions. Many of them bounce back.

That adds up to 60%. What about the other 40%?

Research has shown that it is attributable to voluntary control, activities that are intentional on your behalf. This 40% potential gives you the opportunity for powerful

---

[7] Sonja Lyubomirsky. *The How of Happiness: A Scientific Approach to Getting The Life You Want*

breakthroughs in happiness. How you think and what you do in your daily life drives this 40% of happiness. That's gold.

Recognizing this, doesn't it make sense to review very carefully what you do, how you spend your time? If you closely emulate what very happy people engage in, that could be a game-changer. And that is the thrust of the remainder of this book: How to boost your happiness by capitalizing on the 40%.

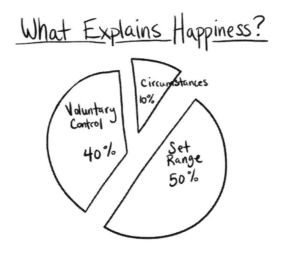

What Explains Happiness?

Voluntary Control 40%

Circumstances 10%

Set Range 50%

What's Your Definition of Happiness?

W hat exactly is happiness? Positive emotions, well-being, something else?

Here's the Google definition:

The state of being happy.

It can mean the most common positive emotions: pleasure, contentment, satisfaction, cheerfulness, merriment, gaiety, joy, joyfulness, joviality, glee, delight, good spirits, lightheartedness, well-being, enjoyment.

Interest   Hope   Awe
      Joy   Serenity

Most Common Positive Emotions

Love   Inspiration

Pride   Gratitude

              Amusement

Happiness is thought of as the good life: Freedom from suffering, flourishing, well-being, joy, prosperity and pleasure. Also consider the 10 most common positive emotions: joy, gratitude, serenity, interest, hope, pride, amusement, inspiration, awe, and love.

Life, liberty and the pursuit of happiness is a fundamental right granted in the Declaration of Independence by the founding fathers.

Ask your family members or a group of friends or co-workers for their definition of happiness. I guarantee you it will be a fascinating discussion.

But what's more important is your definition of happiness. Take a few minutes to reflect on this, and record your thoughts in your logbook.

Happiness has no single definition. The happy person experiences it relatively, what psychologists refer to as "subjective well-being."

As we think about happiness, it's useful to distinguish between momentary pleasure and longer-lasting emotion.

The Pleasant Life

Someone who thinks only about pleasure is a hedonist. The hedonist sees to stack up the pleasurable moments and have as few unhappy times as possible. In his way of thinking, happiness overall is the sum of pleasurable moments less the bad times.

But those who concentrate on seeking pleasure find themselves on a treadmill. As more material possessions and pleasurable moments accumulate, they prove to be less and less fulfilling.

Ultimately, hedonism falls short. Chasing pleasure for the sake of pleasure is the shallowest way to experience happiness, and it lasts only a short time. Most of us seek short-term pleasure, but greater satisfaction and feeling of well-being arises from having *earned* gratification. Undeserved short-term pleasure leads to emptiness over time. Concentrating on pleasure is the pursuit of a Pleasant Life.[8]

---

[8] Martin E.P. Seligman. *Authentic Happiness: Using the New Positive Psychology to Realize Your Potential for Lasting Fulfillment*

The Good Life

To move beyond this, toward true happiness, means elevating well-being by exercising personal strengths and values. You apply your personal strengths and values in your work and home life. Think about how you felt when you learned to play a musical instrument, created art, solved a complex problem with your significant other, or successfully raised a child. You brought your strengths and values to create something of great value, and that gave rise to authentic happiness and gratification. Concentrating on exercising your strengths and values is the pursuit of a Good Life.

The Purposeful Life

To progress further still, pursue a deeply felt purpose, leveraging and developing strengths and values. Living a Purposeful Life means concentrating on a cause bigger than yourself, that gets you out of bed in the morning, excites and ignites you. It's a life of growth, stretch, and reinvention. Trials and tests mark a Purposeful Life, but the dogged devotion to a purpose overwhelms the bad times. The Purposeful Life can be yours if you have the courage to define your purpose and the discipline to pursue it. If you're up for the purpose, I'll show you how.

Which Life is For You?

The Purposeful Life

The Good Life

The Pleasant Life

Chuck Bolton

Virtue[9]

Sweet day, so cool, so calm, so bright,

The bridal of the earth and sky,

The dew shall weep thy fall tonight;

For thou must die.

Sweet rose, whose hue angry and brave

Bids the rash gazer wipe his eye,

Thy root is ever in its grave,

And thou must die.

Sweet spring, full of sweet days and roses,

A box where sweets compacted lie,

My music shows ye have your closes,

And all must die.

Only a sweet and virtuous soul,

Like a seasoned timer, never gives;

But though the whole world turn to coal,

Then chiefly lives.

_____

[9] George Herbert. _Virtue_
http://www.ccel.org/h/herbert/temple/Vertue.html

George Herbert

This poem, nearly 400 years old, by George Herbert, makes the same point, perhaps more eloquently: That only the pursuit of lasting Purpose, and Purposefulness, is ultimately fulfilling. By the way, George Herbert died of tuberculosis before he turned 40; he was a beloved Anglican priest.

My Definition of Happiness

Happiness is committing to and living a Purposeful Life while becoming my best. Happiness is being positive in the the present, having an optimistic outlook toward the future and making sense of and accepting the past.

The Battle between Repeater and Reinventor

There's a conflict inside of each of us: a battle for our happiness. Deep inside of us, there is a part of us that desperately seeks happiness, and a Purposeful Life. But another part of us seeks to take the easy way, and live for short-term pleasure.

In the crazy busy world, we can repeat what we've always done, what we've always believed, and how we've always operated. But we may very well end up languishing, and we sure won't flourish. Our culture and economy feed off of uncertainty and unhappiness. This world sows seeds of discontent, overloading and distracting us, leading us away from our birthright of happiness. Advertisements and commercials try to brain wash us in believing that happiness can be bought. We play defense, instead of offense. This is the Repeater version of ourselves. The not-so-happy version.

Also inside each of us is a happy self, a hero in our journey, successful, bold, focused, with the courage to accept the call of living happily. This is the Reinventor. This self is comfortable with discovery, growth, and reinvention.

The good news is you can reinvent yourself to happiness, to become the successful, happy person you were meant to be. To reinvent, you'll need a straightforward, practical system to follow. This book describes a holistic system you can apply to reinvent your life for happiness and success. You'll do yourself a great favor. And you'll be a role model – a positive example – to others you touch.[10]

Now, it's time to discover the five critical steps for reinventing your happiness.

---

[10] Chuck Bolton. *The Reinvented Leader: Five Critical Steps to Becoming Your Best*

The 5 Steps to Reinvent Your Happiness

5 Steps to Happiness

1) Reinvent Mindset
2) Reinvigorate Relationships
3) Develop Happiness Skills
4) Reclaim Energy, Then Time
5.) Training vs. Trying

Step 1: Reinvent Your Mindset

First, train your mind. Repeaters stick with what is pleasant in the moment. This causes happiness to wane over time. The Reinventor who lives the Purposeful Life also enjoys pleasure, but concentrates on gratification, which lasts longer, because of the effort required to achieve it. Repeaters quit learning and adapting, and have fallen into a fixed mindset, so that they solve tomorrow's problems with yesterday's solutions. They maintain limiting beliefs that hinder their ability to grow, be happy and succeed.

Reinventors have a growth mindset: the will to learn and apply new skills; they adopt empowering beliefs.

Step 2: Reinvigorate Your Relationships

When you reinvent your happiness, you learn to appreciate and develop your relationships with others. The happiest people have rich relationships. More than 70% of happiness is driven by the strength and energy of your relationships.

Step 3: Develop Your Happiness Skills

Reinventors are lifelong learners, constantly applying new knowledge and skills.

Implementing the eight happiness skills, proven to raise your well-being, resilience and fulfillment, giving you the keys to living a purposeful life and sustaining your happiness.

Step 4: Reclaim Your Energy, then Your Time

In today's crazy busy world, you need energy to thrive and flourish. Tapping into and renewing the four sources of energy gives you the fuel to get your work done and engage in those activities and relationships that most make you happy. Much can be done to increase your physical, mental, emotional and spiritual energy. Reinventors expend and renew their energy; Repeaters squander their energy.

Step 5: Train, Don't just Try

Knowledge doesn't equal change. We overestimate what we can do by trying, underestimate what we can do by training. Repeaters try. They'll continue only as long as they're interested. Reinventors train, like world-class athletes. They embrace deliberate practice, a daily routine, and new habits to raise their happiness. They build new skills. They get better and better, happier and happier.

Step 1:
Reinvent Your Mindset

Let God transform
us into new people by
changing the way we think.
— Romans 12:2

Increasing your happiness starts with your mind.

How you view the world and think about yourself have a profound effect on how you lead your life. You examine and adjust your mindset and beliefs as needed.

What's Your Mindset?

Your mindset is your worldview. It's your way of thinking that determines your outlook, attitude, and behavior. Your mindset is an important part of your character. Fortunately, you can change it.

2 Mindsets

Fixed

Growth

Mindsets come in two flavors: fixed and growth. In some parts of life, you may have a growth mindset, while you may have a fixed mindset in others.

People with a fixed mindset believe their qualities, personalities, strengths and weaknesses are set at an early age. Either you're good at something, or bad. Someone with a fixed mindset might say: "I'm bad at math. Everyone in my family has been bad at math. I'll never be good at math. Therefore, I'm not capable of learning or enjoying math."

Or, "My Mother has never been a happy person. I guess my gloom is something I've inherited from her."

People with fixed mindsets don't enjoy learning; they lack curiosity. They hit a brick wall. They often prejudge their capabilities and potential. They get impatient for results; they need instant gratification. They believe "You can't teach an old dog new tricks." They are half-hearted, at best, in trying to learn new skills. They fail to appreciate that intentional, deliberate practice is required to get desired outcomes.

People with growth mindsets believe a person's full potential is unknowable. They know that, with passion, training and commitment, virtually anyone can build talents and capabilities. They love to learn. They see challenges as opportunities to stretch. They don't let setbacks discourage them. Instead, they accept challenges, learn from failures, and continue trying to improve their performance. They have the will to learn the skill.

Athletes and performers need growth mindsets to thrive. Although Michael Jordan was cut from his high school basketball team, he went on to become perhaps the best basketball player ever. Entertainers such as Madonna and Elton John have reinvented themselves to stay in the spotlight, at the top of the music industry, for decades. You need to do the same.

To become your best as a person, to raise your level of happiness, reflect on your mindset. You may need to change it.

In each of the eight slices of the Wheel of Happiness, are you operating with a growth or fixed mindset? In which do you need to move to a growth mindset, to live a more balanced life? Recognizing this, you can begin thinking and operating in ways that are more productive for you. How about at work? Are there topics where you need a growth mindset? Back to your logbook. It's time to reflect on these questions. Start writing about the mindset you operate with for each key slice of life.

Beliefs: Limiting or Empowering?

What separates unhappy people from happy ones? Often, it is the difference between a limiting belief and an empowering one. Beliefs are important: a driving force in our lives, that can work for or against us. Becoming aware of your beliefs, and determining if they are empowering or self-defeating, is crucial to becoming your best.

Your mindset is like the canopy of an umbrella. Under that umbrella, providing support, metal ribs and stretchers connect the umbrella's shaft to the handle. Think of them as beliefs, and the canopy of the umbrella as your mindset—which protects you. It allows you to face challenges and opportunities. The ribs and stretchers, the beliefs, give the canopy support.

Beliefs are formed in two ways. The first is teaching. For example, throughout your youth, perhaps you were taught, *"Happiness comes only after hard work."* The second is experience. Often, our beliefs come to us reflexively – we've often never actually defined them.

Beliefs are like muscles. They become stronger with exercise: Thinking, writing and talking about them. This takes time and reflection. By reflecting on them, you can discard the ones that don't serve you well, while keeping those that fit with the leader you seek to become.

To create clarity, defining hour beliefs is useful. Limiting beliefs come in three kinds:

If/Then … "If I don't get promoted to Vice President by the time I'm 30, then I'll never become the success I want to be…"

Meaning … "Carrying the extra 10 pounds makes me unattractive, unlovable and unhappy."

Identity … "I'm a perfectionist, and know that no one else can do that task so well."

Chuck Bolton

Once we form a belief, we tend to stick with it. Often, we form them early in life. How do we know if a belief still fits us? Just because our experience has borne out a particular belief so far, doesn't necessarily mean that it will continue to.

How can you "smoke out" your limiting beliefs? Ask yourself whether each of them is useful. If not, choose ones that work better for you. Look at the Wheel of Happiness again. Are there areas where you're not satisfied? Why? Chances are, it's because of a limiting belief. For example, if you're not in the physical condition you know you should be in, what are your beliefs about exercise? About eating? Chances are your beliefs around these topics could be more empowering.

Performance breakthroughs always begin with a change of beliefs. That means replacing limiting beliefs with new, empowering ones. Listen to your self-talk, and think about context.

Can you adopt empowering beliefs that fit your experience, and make you feel hopeful about meeting your challenges? Developing empowering beliefs requires three steps:

1. Write them down. A great way to define a belief is to reflect on the future you are working to create. What do you value and stand for? When you define beliefs from an aspirational perspective, you give yourself and other people something to believe in! Using the term, "I envision..." is a great prompt.

2. Ask, do my beliefs limit or empower me?

3. Identify a limiting belief, and change it into an empowering belief. What's the opposite of that belief? Could the opposite work for you?

For example:

Limiting belief: "I've seen that change can be risky, so I'd rather play it safe."

Empowering belief: "Even if I run into challenges when dealing with change, there's always a way to meet them, when I'm committed."

Limiting belief: "I can't regularly exercise, because I can't commit to making time for it. I've got to be able to react to emergencies."

Empowering belief: "I will go to bed at 10, so I can get up at 6, and exercise 45 minutes to start the day. That leaves enough time to get to the office by 8."

Limiting belief: "I don't have time to teach and coach others to do this task, so I'll just do it myself."

Empowering belief: "When I choose to do a task I could show and ask others to do, I over-manage and under-lead. One of my responsibilities as a parent is to teach and coach, even if my child doesn't complete the task exactly like I would."

Limiting belief: "It's impossible to be happy, with everything moving so fast."

Empowering belief: "This is a time of great opportunity and growth. I need to remember to take control of my energy and time and intentionally construct my own happiness."

Limiting belief: "If I keep my nose to the grindstone, everything will turn out OK, and I'll be happy then."

Empowering belief: "Nobody is responsible for my success and happiness except me. I am responsible for changing what's necessary, and creating my own future and enjoying happiness in the present."

Empowering Beliefs to Increase Happiness

1. The past doesn't have to determine the future.

2. Happiness is a learned skill.

3. I can control much of my happiness through my beliefs and actions.

4. I can always choose happiness.

"Failure isn't fatal, but failure to change might be."

- John Wooden

Step 2:
Re-Invigorate Your Relationships

What is the one thing that extremely happy people do differently: The big kahuna of happiness? They have a rich repertoire of relationships. They are extremely social.

Many studies have shown that social relationships are the antidote for depression and boost happiness, success, and high performance. For example, in a 1996 study, researchers Murray and Peacock found, "Contrary to the belief that happiness is hard to explain, or that it depends on having great wealth, researchers have identified the core factors in a happy life. The primary components are number of friends, closeness of friends, closeness of family and relationships with co-workers and neighbors. Together these features explain about 70% of personal happiness."

It's not good to be alone. We thrive when we connect with others. Otherwise, we languish. Those who are emotionally isolated are more prone to loneliness, depression, anxiety, self-esteem, substance abuse, and eating and sleeping disorders. They are more likely to give in, to default to The Pleasant Life and abandon the path toward The Purposeful Life.

Despite the importance of friendships in improving happiness, three trends in relationships are disheartening:

1. Emotional distance is increasing. Our workload, fast pace, many distractions, and other factors cause emotional distance. Even though you may communicate electronically, perhaps as Facebook friends, you may be emotionally distant-- even if you're close by.

2.   Energy level in our relationships is decreasing.

Energy is what creates great marriages, families, partnerships, teams, and companies. What's the energy level in your relationships? Is it trending up or down?

Earlier you used the Wheel of Happiness to assess the current satisfaction of your key relationships. On a scale of 1 to 10, you rated your current satisfaction with your spouse/partner, children, extended family, and friends. What about people at work - your boss, peers, direct reports, key clients or customers, suppliers, consultants?

What can you do to energize and strengthen these important relationships?

3. Critical relationships are becoming fewer (and sometimes more fragile).

Thirty years ago, the American Sociological Review reported Americans had on average three people in whom to confide important matters. That dropped to two as of 2006. Twenty-five percent have no one to turn to. Too many are not investing face-to-face time to create and maintain deep connections.

Need to expand your friendships? Here are a few ideas:

Timeless Wisdom for Making Friends

Nearly 80 years ago, Dale Carnegie, American writer and lecturer on self-improvement and interpersonal skills, shared simple advice in his book **How to Win Friends and Influence People**, which has sold 15 million copies worldwide. His six ways to make people like you are still valid today. [11]They are:

---

[11] Dale Carnegie. *How to Win Friends and Influence People*

1. Become genuinely interested in others.

2. Smile.

3. Remember and use the other person's name. To that person, the sweetest and most important sound in any language is hearing his name.

4. Be a good listener and encourage others to talk about themselves.

5. Talk in terms of other people's interests.

6. In a sincere way, make the other person feel important.

Carnegie said, "You can make more friends in two weeks by becoming a good listener than you can in two years trying to get people interested in you."

Do you follow these principles? Which ones can you do a better job on, in your relationships?

Maximum Generosity

What do those who maintain robust relationships do differently from others? How do they succeed in developing them? It's more than just likability. They're exceptionally generous. Building relationships, connecting, takes being generous and intimate.

According to the Merriam-Webster Dictionary, generosity is the quality of being kind, understanding, and not selfish.

Can you be more generous? What if you led that way? Think about how you'd help others, and receive the satisfaction of knowing you'd helped. It's never too late.

What do generous people ask others? Instead of, "How are you?" they say, "What's the story?"—a common way to greet people in Ireland. This opens up the possibility for a rich discussion and connection.

"What's the story?" means "What's going on? What's up? Tell me what's important to you – right now." You get to share your wants, needs, and desires, to be understood. That's something everyone wants.

Generous people ask other powerful questions, too. Here are several:

- What's most exciting to you now?

- What gets you up in the morning?

- What's keeping you up at night?

- What's on your agenda?

- What's the most important thing we should discuss?

- What will it take for this to be a successful year for you?

- What's your greatest dream?

- What's your biggest accomplishment this week?

- What will be your biggest accomplishment next week?

Generosity is more than asking the right question. It's being present. It's doing what's right for the other person. When you lead with generosity, you make an enormous, indelible impact on others.

Whose lives are you bettering today, because of your generosity? Whose list will you be on? Write those names down, too.

You have mandatory meetings in your calendar, but do you have mandatory time for friends? Do you have scheduled friend time? Too many people don't.

Who's Made the Extra Difference in Your Life?

Think about the people in your life who've had a profound influence on you--who took a personal interest, showed that they cared. They could be your parents, grandparents, aunts and uncles, teachers, coaches, friends, clergy, bosses, co-workers, or others. Perhaps someone who saw potential in you that you couldn't see. Or gave you a second chance, even if you didn't deserve it.

Several people made a huge difference in my life.

My Aunt Vivian. Through her love and kindness, she brought closer a small extended family, who had experienced too many deaths during a short span of years. For her listening, for her roast beef dinners and German chocolate cakes. For playing games with the kids. For her contagious happiness and optimism.

John LaSage, my Babe Ruth League baseball coach. A winner who taught us to respect the game as 13-year olds, and showed us how professional baseball players wore the uniform and carried themselves--and demanded we do the same. For his patience, compassion and his inspiration to us. We were the worst team in the league, but as 14-year-olds, he made us champions. He showed us how.

For Brother Frank Walsh and Arthur Flodstrom, college professors who touched my heart, and challenged me to develop my mind and think big.

For Bob DeBaun, who taught me what it was to be a leader. The coaching and advice he provided during our commuting made an enormous difference in my career. Bob passed away way too young of multiple myeloma.

How about you? Take a moment to write down in your logbook the names of those who inspired you. What's their common denominator?

For sure, it's generosity. They were generous in every way possible. They asked about your hopes, desires, and goals. When you met with them, do you remember receiving their full attention, like you were the only other person in the world? They make up your "most generous" list.

As you reflect on people who have had a profound influence on you, write down what each of them did that affected you so much. Write each a letter. Better yet, call or visit them to thank them, and share your letter personally – a gratitude visit. It will be a profound moment for you both.

While you're at it, check out this short video about reaching out to these friends from Soul Pancake – The Science of Gratitude:[12]

https://www.youtube.com/watch?v=oHv6vTKD6lgh

It offers some useful ideas on how to make this a magical moment. For those who took the time to write the note, but couldn't make a phone call or visit, their happiness grew 2%-4%. For those who telephoned, happiness increased 4 and 19%. Expressing gratitude will make you happier. The biggest jump in happiness was for the one who was least happy. So, if you are having a tough time, this activity will have an even bigger impact for you.

The Small Group

How can you be part of a group of others who genuinely care for and support one another? In **Think and Grow Rich,** Napoleon Hill introduced what he described as mastermind groups: peer support groups consist of like-minded peers who support, brainstorm, challenge, and hold you accountable to achieve your personal and professional goals.

Similarly, you can create a group of 8 – 12 people who "have your back:" act as your ardent supporters professionally, serve as peers--a board of advisors.

Bill George, Harvard Business School professor, best-selling author, and former CEO of Medtronic, describes what he calls True North Groups: "The challenges we face these days are so great that we cannot rely entirely on ourselves, our

---

[12] The Science of Happiness video – *An Experiment in Gratitude – SoulPancake*

communities, or our organizations to support us and help us stay on track. We need a small group of people with whom we can have in-depth discussions and share intimately about the most important things in our lives – our happiness and sadness, our hopes and fears, our beliefs and convictions."[13]

Not having a small group (or two) leaves you alone in the wilderness. They can stretch you, and keep you growing, focused, and connected. Small groups are a must for reinvention.

Have you ever visited a McDonald's at 7 a.m. on two consecutive days? What do you see? The same group of seniors, faithfully socializing together.

Those regulars at McDonald's are an informal small group. For you, too, having a small group of friends outside of immediate family is extremely important.

My small group is 10 men who I've met with for six years, Saturday mornings at 8. We share life, encourage one another, celebrate, and tackle life's challenges. We discuss books, do volunteer projects, and take weekend retreats twice a year, all while deepening our faith. This is an intimate, safe, committed group, in which all matters of the heart and head are shared. Our fellowship and care raises the happiness and well-being of each of us.

What's A Day Like For...?

If you work with others in a department or a team, chances are some of the relationships between team members are good, some just OK, others not so great.

---

[13] Bill George. *True North Groups: A Powerful Path to Personal and Leadership Development*

Taking a little time to encourage collegial relationships among team members pays dividends and makes everyone happier.

To raise awareness and empathy, and strengthen relationships among team members, a powerful activity is the "What's a Day Like For...?"

Suppose the team has six members: the leader, and five direct reports who head up Sales & Marketing, Operations, R&D, Finance, and Human Resources. For each, four flip chart pages are created: Highs, Lows, Rewards, and Frustrations.

The sales & marketing manager is excused from the conference room, and asked to summarize his highs, lows, rewards and frustrations. The leader and the other four put themselves in the shoes of the sales and marketing head. They write their perceptions of his highs, lows, rewards, and frustrations on their flip charts.

When the sales & marketing manager returns, the group compares his list with theirs.

Often, the discussion is rich and revealing. It's not uncommon for the team to learn their views are often very different than his. The result is a shared understanding and strengthening of relationships, and other breakthroughs, too.

The exercise is repeated for each member of the team, including the team leader.

Practicing the 90-Second Rule

When you return home at night after a day of work, how do you greet your family? I have to admit that I've been guilty of bringing a hard day at work home with me. But since being introduced to Jim Fannin's The 90-Second Rule video, I'm doing my best to change.[14]

http://tinyurl.com/lzgrzv

Fannin's premise is: "If you've been away for more than two hours, the first 90 seconds you spend with someone is more important to the quality of the relationship than spending time with them for hours later." In other words, clear your mind, and prepare to fully engage with the people at home.

Fannin suggests you "mirror" your significant other. If she's happy, you bask in that; if she's sad, you meet her there, and try to pull her up. It's such little things that show others how you care about and value them. A way to get connected, aligned and raise the happiness of all.

Take a Page From a Fortune 500 Company

If your children are home, and you want to raise them into exemplary adults, consider taking a page or two from big business. With hectic schedules, family life often gets the short end of the stick. Here are a few ideas to help you raise happy, emotionally healthy children.

Research shows that family meals make a huge difference in the lives of kids. A University of Michigan study discovered the amount of time children spent eating meals at home was the single biggest predictor of better academic achievement and fewer behavioral problems.

It's OK if you can't get everyone together for dinner--it can be any meal. Just making it a priority and getting everyone around the table as often as possible is the main thing.

---

[14] Jim Fannin. *The 90 Second Rule* http://tinyurl.com/lzgrzv

Holding a weekly family meeting is another opportunity to bring everyone together. It can be done around the dinner table – perhaps on a Sunday night. The agenda: what's gone well this week, what didn't go so well, what do we work on next week? What are the big developments?

What about creating a family mission statement? Setting aside some time to discuss what your family stands for, what it means to be part of your family. It's defining your family values.

Here's an example:

"We want to be a family that both serves and has fun. We'll schedule an evening a month to volunteer at the church or a non-profit, and an evening at least weekly that's a family fun night. "

And how about a family vision for the upcoming year? What if you took some time at one of the Sunday night family meetings to do a little envisioning? It's an opportunity to create, plan for, and invest in shared family experiences.

Here's how you might get that started. It's January 2018, and, as our family looks back at 2017, it's been a really great year for us. But like every year, we face challenges-- some ups and downs, but more ups than downs. As we look back, what did we accomplish and celebrate together? (Consider using the Wheel of Happiness to explore in a more detailed way.)

For example:

How did we serve others together?

What did we accomplish together?

What fun did we have together?

What family events and experiences did we enjoy?

Did we schedule time to vacation or do fun things?

What did we learn together?

What went well? What could have gone better?

What will be our plans for the next year?

Knowing your Family History

Research shows that a child's knowing his family history is the #1 predictor his well-being. In **The Secret of Happy Families**, author Bruce Feiler shares, researchers at Emory University did a study that showed that the kids who know more about their family history had a greater belief that they could control their world and a higher degree of self-confidence. "It was the number one predictor of a child's emotional well-being." [15]

Just over one year ago, we lost a dear aunt in our family, Aunt Phyllis. With her passing, among my mother, her four siblings, and their spouses only one aunt survives. My mother's parents were Swedish immigrants who met and married in Chicago in the early 1900s. My grandfather was a carpenter and contractor. My grandmother was a housewife. They had five children and nine grandchildren.

My nine cousins, with their significant others/spouses and their children, the second cousins, have spread out over 12

---

[15] Bruce Feiler. *The Secret of Happy Families: Improve Your Mornings, Tell Your Family History, Fight Smarter, Go Out and Play, and Much More*

states. Our extended family includes a total of 55 people, and, spread out geographically, busy as we are, we rarely all get together.

Immediately after Aunt Phyllis' passing, we created a private Facebook group, to share pictures and to communicate with one another. Nearly 35 family members joined it. In the first few months since we created the page, more than 150 photos have been posted along with hundreds of comments. We've relived weddings, Christmases, and family reunions. We've shared the family history with our children and their children. We've gone to our attics and basements and to dig out the old scrapbooks and photos and to share memories. We've also discussed the deaths and tough times, and how the family overcame adversity. We're spreading good feelings when we connect and exchange our memories of family celebrations 40-50 years ago.

Every few days or so, someone shares a photo of the past that gets everyone exchanging comments and giggling. We're showing our children they have a bigger family than just their immediate families. And when we connect, we bless one another and we are each blessed, too. A good thing indeed.

Keeping the family tight, using Facebook in our private group, feels like a good use of technology. It's brought us closer and helped make us happier. We even planned and held a reunion in Chicago during the summer of 2016. For each of us, it was one of the highlights of the year.

Now, more than ever, in this crazy busy world, we need tight relationships to survive and thrive. It's especially true for when times are tough. What is too often the response when adversity hits? Hunker down and go it alone. Here's the bottom line: you should never worry alone.

Step 3:
Develop The Eight Happiness Skills

To increase your happiness long-term, know and apply the happiness skills. Mastery of these skills will be crucial to your happiness reinvention.

#1: Live Your "Why"

Have you ever met someone at a social event who asked you, "So, what do you do?" That's a challenging question for most people. Maybe what you are paid for isn't how you define yourself. Or maybe you are in transition, or not so happy with your job.

The truth is, people really care less what you do, than why you do it. And to live a purposeful live, you'll want to explicitly define and clarify this.

What exactly is your "why?" It's the unique difference you seek to make in the world. It's the reason you get out of bed in the morning, to do what you do. Your "why" should excite you and inspire you. It's a challenge bigger than you. It's the pursuit that motivates you. It serves as your North Star; it's your course, speaks deeply to your soul, your "I Have a Dream" belief. If it doesn't, you haven't found it yet.

Unfortunately, too many never define this. As a result, they drift. They lead only the Pleasant Life. What about you?

How do you define your "why?" Get quiet, look deep into your heart, and identify what you're really passionate about. Self-awareness and reflection is required to be certain you're hearing and following your heart, not just your ego. When you follow your heart, you'll tap into your passions. You'll create a purpose around what you love. That will give you greater energy, creativity and happiness. You'll feel alive.

A few years ago, I was referred by a client who had a colleague, John, a president of a business unit of a healthcare services firm. When my client spoke with John about the work we had done together to lift the capability of his leadership team, John was interested in learning more and asked for an introduction.

When I met with John, he told me he ran a successful business that was growing, a division of a large publicly-traded company, and had been in his role for four years. The corporation had grown in revenue and earnings significantly in the past three years, and the value of John's stock options had jumped. John had an important leadership role, and appeared to have a bright future. John seemed to be a fortunate man.

However, when I had two meetings with John at his office, he was critical of the commitment and capability of several of the executives reporting to him. He also questioned the capability and the strategic direction of the CEO and other senior corporate leaders. He felt he should have been promoted earlier in the year to a group executive role; the way he described his position at the company, it was clear he felt he was being treated unfairly. He said he was undercompensated; he could easily make more if he went elsewhere.

After our first meeting, I thought John might just have been having a bad day. But it was apparent after the second meeting that John was "toxic." That is, he wasn't interested in learning how to become a more inspiring leader, in transforming his executives in a cohesive team of leaders who were committed to becoming their best, to creating a great organization.

Instead, he was self-absorbed and miserable. It was all about John. To him, his important leadership role was only a job.

Contrast that with the receptionist at John's office, a woman named Patricia: She was friendly, outgoing, and professional. Walking through the entrance for my first meeting, she smiled. "Welcome to our company. How are you? How can I help you today?" While signing me in, she asked questions about my day. After calling John's assistant to inform her about my arrival, she discussed how much she loved working the company and drew inspiration from the company's mission: improving healthcare access and outcomes. She was engaging, a terrific sales person for the company.

On my second visit to see John, a few weeks after the first, Patricia greeted me again by name. I asked her, "Patricia, what do you see your job as here?" She said, "I'm the #1 ambassador. When someone walks through that door for the first time – whether a visitor, or an interviewee or whoever – their first impression of us is the quality of the interaction with me. I treat others the way I want to be treated, the way I expect to be treated. I love this company and my role. I play an important role in our success." It was clear Patricia had thought carefully about her role and her contribution.

John the president vs. Patricia the receptionist. John saw his role as a job. Patricia saw hers as a calling. John didn't have a "why," Patricia did. John was miserable. Patricia was happy. We need more Patricias in this world.

Here are questions to help you find your why:

1. What do you love to do? What are you absolutely qualified to teach others? If you truly commit yourself with heart, head, and hands, what can you do best? Where can you make a significant contribution?

2. Who do you do it for?

3. What do they need or want?

4. What are the emotions you want others to experience, when they interact with you?

5. How do they change, as a result of what you give them?

The emphasis in the five questions is on others, not within yourself. The most happy and successful people devote themselves on serving others. Creating happiness for others makes us happy, too.

Now, write your answers in your logbook. Keep them brief and to the point. Twitter limits you to 140 characters, and that's a good limit for this, too. Consider using either of the following templates:

I wake up every day inspired to _____ *so that* _____.

or

I help _____ *do* _____, *even if* _____.

<u>My "Why"</u>: I wake up every day inspired to help leaders, their teams, and companies reinvent, to become their best, so they can achieve great results, and have a meaningful impact on the world.

Many people spend their whole lives trying to find their "why." But you've just learned how to identify yours. Now do it! Living your "why" is a tool for happiness and "future-proofing" yourself. It's a prerequisite to becoming your best.

Living your why, while exercising your signature strengths, is a pathway to becoming a butterfly, even if you feel like a caterpillar for now.

Those signature strengths help you turbocharge your "why." Every one of us is blessed with some. When we pursue our "why," using our signature strengths daily, it produces authentic happiness and gratification. It's the secret to experiencing "flow."

What are your top five signature strengths? Take a free survey to find out at: viasurvey.org.

#2: Practice Gratefulness Daily

We all know people who have everything, but are unhappy. Other people have had misfortunes, suffered many adversities, but are deeply happy. How can this be? Because the latter are grateful. It's not that happiness makes them grateful. That's putting it backwards. Gratefulness makes them happy.

Gratitude affects your brain biochemistry. Feeling grateful activates dopamine in your brain stem, which makes you feel good. Grateful people are joyful people. According to Robert Emmon, Ph.D., professor of psychology and a positive psychology scholar, regular grateful thinking can increase happiness by at least 25%.[16]

Thinking of the things you are grateful for requires you to dwell on the positive aspects of your life. Taking the time to be grateful for all the good things is a great way to change your perspective. It's appreciation in the "now." When you are grateful, you are happy.

---

[16] Robert Emmons. *Gratitude Works! The Science and Practice of Saying Thanks*

Why do we neglect something so basic as being grateful? Because we don't slow down and think. To live a Purposeful Life, build gratitude practice into your daily routine.

Here's the absolute best question to ask yourself daily to sustain your high level of happiness:

"What am I grateful for?"

Gratefulness - 5 Magic Words Daily

What am I grateful for...?

Every day, when you wake up, spend five minutes thinking deeply about the last 24 hours. List three things you are grateful for in your logbook. I use a separate logbook as my Gratitude Journal. Journaling the three (or sometimes more) top-of-mind topics I'm most grateful for that morning is a cornerstone of my daily routine.

As you think about them, reflect on the vision you have for your day. How do you want to see it go? How will you present yourself to others? How do you want to be embraced by the world? Who is depending on you? Be clear about living your "why" with a positive intention. Be more grateful to become happier.

#3: Visualize a Happy, Successful Day

When Michael Phelps, the most decorated Olympian of all time (with a total of 28 medals, including 23 golds – double the second-highest record holders – over four Olympiads), prepares for a race, he visualizes every moment of it: standing on the block, diving into the water, and every stroke until he touches the wall ahead of everyone else. He positively anticipates a victory.

The brain can't distinguish between an actual event, and a well-crafted vision of a successful performance. If you've done the prep work, imagining the event and outcome well enough, it will likely come true. Of course, this works for bad events, too, so be careful what you envision.

Phelps and other elite athletes and world-class performers create a positive video clip they run over and over again in their minds. It never includes a negative outcome.

How does this apply to you? Prepare yourself to carry out your "why" with aplomb. Take the time each day to visualize, to anticipate, a successful, happy, outstanding performance. Anticipate your daily activities with positive expectations. Believe you will be happy and successful. Visualize your happiness. Visualize your success.   Reinvent your beliefs. Ban doubt in your mind. See yourself as a masterpiece. Your happiness drives success. And you have the method to flourish!

For we are God's masterpiece.
He has created us anew in
Christ Jesus, so we can do
the good things he planned
for us long ago.
— Ephesians 2:10

Pull out your logbook. *What's your vision of a happy and successful day today?*

#4: What Inspires and Makes You Happy?

"Every day, do
Something you love."
— George Burns

Getting yourself to feel positive is fuel for happiness, as happiness is not only a feeling, but a desired state. Knowing the positive emotions is a good start in experiencing them more often. They are: joy, gratitude, serenity, interest, hope, pride, amusement, inspiration, awe and love.

In the pursuit of the Purposeful Life, you'll need inspiration, and undoubtedly, you'll inspire others. What inspires you? When we're inspired, it's more than pleasure: it's a spirit-based word meaning that something has been breathed into us. We're in-spirit. Inspiration lifts our spirits. We flourish when we're inspired.

Which sources of inspiration resonate most for you? They include:

- Creating – making something new;

- Reflecting – meditating, praying, solitary thinking;

- Reading—studying and learning;

- Serving—helping others;

- Relating—one-on-one, or in small groups where relationships can blossom;

- Worshipping – deep feeling when praise and adoration are given voice; and

- Acting – Passion to act or perform, maybe to correct an injustice or take advantage of an opportunity.

7 Sources of Inspiration
- Creating
- Reflecting
- Reading
- Serving
- Relating
- Worshipping
- Acting

Pull out your logbook. What sources do you find most inspiring? Can you rank your sources of inspiration from most to least? How can you feel yourself more inspired?

#5: Avoid the "When/Then…"

Have you ever had a dialogue with yourself, that went something like this?

"When I get an "A" in the class, then I'll be happy."

"When I make the team or get the part, then I'll be happy."

"When that attractive person likes me and we start dating, then I'll be happy."

"When I get into that college, then I'll be happy"

"When I get that job, then I'll be happy."

"When I get married, then I'll be happy."

"When I lose 10 pounds, then I'll be happy."

"When I can afford to buy that car, then I'll be happy."

"When I can get that promotion, and buy a bigger house, then I'll be happy."

If you are like most of us, you have your share of *"When this happens, then I'll be happy"* thoughts. Perhaps you were taught that happiness was the reward for work. After you earned the "A", you'd be happy. If you kept your nose to the grindstone, and behaved yourself, you'd have happiness at the finish line waiting for you.

And then when you achieved that goal, you felt good – for a short while – but it faded. It wasn't sustainable. You missed the chance to be happy in the present.

But happiness is not something you have to earn; it's something that you deserve. Visualize your happiness and success. Pay attention to the trick the ego plays on you when you engage in the *"When/Then"* line of self-talk.

Happiness is there for you, at any time and at any moment. It's your choice. Choose to be happy in the present, visualize and be optimistic about the future, and look forward to what is coming your way. Don't fall for the *"When/Then"* fallacy.

#6: Write Your Powerful Personal Story

More important than what actually happens to us is the way we look at our lives.

Happy people and unhappy people's lives, objectively, are not all that different. Instead, surveys show that happy and unhappy people tend to have had very similar experiences.

The *100 Simple Secrets of Happy People* points out that happy people do not experience one success after another. Nor do unhappy people face one failure after another. [17]

The difference is that the average unhappy person spends more than twice as much time thinking about unpleasant events, while happy people tend to seek and rely upon information that brightens their personal outlook. **Source: Lyubomirsky 1994.**

So, what's the best way to make sense of your experiences? To look at your life with perspective and hope?

It's taking the time to write your life story, your "Who am I?" story, about how you've overcome adversity, handled life's ups and downs, to become the person you are today. Writing your personal life story heals wounds and fills you with gratitude toward people who've touched your heart.

Telling your story to those close to you strengthens your bond with them and allows you to inspire them to write and tell their stories. You'll lift their hearts with your story.

Storytelling isn't new. It's baked into our DNA. Paintings on the walls of the Lascaux Caves in the Pyrenees Mountains, 35,000 years old, are the earliest evidence of storytelling.

Tell a great story, others will follow. They get to know you. They come to trust you.

Your story is the connective tissue that draws others to you. Your personal, "*Who am I?*" story, that tells how you overcame adversity, and how that experience is relevant today.

---

[17] David Niven. *The 100 Simple Secrets of Happy People: What Scientists Have Learned and How You Can Use it.*

"Those who tell the stories rule society."
-Plato

To inspire is to tell a story, so as to trigger emotion. Want to thrive? Dig for, write, and tell stories. Build on what you created in #1, Live Your "Why." Help others understand what is important to you, how your life experiences have made you what are today, why you do what you do.

When you master and share your story, you lead a exciting, uplifting journey. It's the most generous thing you can do. When you tell it with conviction and authenticity, you'll hold your audience's attention like a magnet. You'll have a powerful effect--far more interesting and exciting than any PowerPoint presentation. You'll inspire. You'll lead. But you can't do it half-assed. When you tell your story, you've got to be all-in.

How do you write your "Who Am I" story? Get out your logbook, turn on some soft music, get into a reflective frame of mind, and answer the following questions:

1. What are the 10 most fascinating things about you?

2. What qualifies you as an expert?

3. What makes you human?

4. What are your beliefs?

5. What problem do you solve, and why?

6. What were the three most salient events in your life, that have made you the person you are?

7. What was the single most defining moment in your life?

8. What's the single biggest problem, challenge, or opportunity you face today? How is your story relevant to today's situation? How can you use the struggle you faced and journey you walked in the past, to lead today, and in the future?

Write as fast as you can--no critiques or edits for now. Set your timer for 45 minutes. Start with your single most defining moment. Create your one true sentence. My one true sentence: *"Every day, when I was 8 years old, I played a game of catch with my Dad."*

Keep writing. When you finish, read your story out loud. Edit where necessary. Then, record it, and play it back for yourself. Continue tightening it up.

Your story is the story of a hero. You faced a challenge, struggled through it, and ultimately resolved it.

"Scratch the surface in a typical boardroom and we're all just cavemen with briefcases, hungry for a wise person to tell us stories."

Alan Kay, Co-founder of Xerox PARC

Tell it to people who care about you. Get their impressions. Look for ways to relate it to your current situation. Your listeners will be fascinated with your story.

You've got to love your story, tell it with absolute conviction, with every ounce of your being. Never discount or underestimate its power. Practice telling it. Master it. Once you do, you'll want to create more. Go for it! Love it. You are on your way to inspiring others.

So, write your *"Who am I?"* story, in 45 minutes. Then tell it in five minutes, with passion, and without notes, to someone else. That's stretching yourself.

Then, go edit the story. Cut out whatever is unnecessary. Come back the following day, and tell it in three minutes.

Now, tell that story to a few people you feel safe with--who will be supportive, but give you honest feedback. Let them know who you are, and what you stand for. Describe the adversity you've been through, and how it applies today.

Keep rehearsing your story, on the treadmill or exercise bike, or while you're commuting. Soon, you'll be prepared to tell a story that grabs—and moves--hearts and minds!

"The highest-paid person in the first half of this century will be the storyteller. All professionals, including advertisers, teachers, entrepreneurs, politicians, athletes and religious leaders, will be valued for their ability to create stories that will captivate their Audiences."
— Rolf Jensen, Director of the Copenhagen Institute for Future Studies

To see my "Who am I?" story, click here:

https://www.youtube.com/watch?v=u4AsSD6moGA

To thrive in the 21st century depends on your ability to write and tell your story. You'll inspire yourself. You'll increase your happiness. You'll inspire and make others happy, too.

#7: Overcoming Adversity: The ABC's

Everyone experiences adversity. Why is it that some people can bounce back after a devastating illness or personal loss – a big setback – and regain happiness quickly? While others experience what appears to be a small bump in the road, yet seem to be paralyzed, unable to move forward?

To this, it helps to know your ABCs:

What determines how we feel and act in adversity? Our beliefs.[18]

It's our beliefs about adversity that drives the consequences we experience. Beliefs are our immediate emotional reactions to an adverse event. For example, my friend Cal lost his job as a vice president of a large financial institution. His belief: He couldn't understand why he was laid off, and feared he would never get another comparable job, or recoup his income.

The consequences for Cal: A feeling of panic! Bad things will happen. Loss of standing. What will people think? "I'll lose my income. Eventually I'll lose my home, savings and other assets. As an unemployed loser, my wife will no longer love me, my children will be ashamed of me, and I'll end up alone and destitute." Cal's inner dialogue dragged him down.

Now, if Cal's reaction sounds a bit extreme, maybe you've never been the sole breadwinner with big family

---

[18] Karen Reivich and Andrew Shatte. *The Resilience Factor: Seven Essential Skills for Overcoming Life's Inevitable Obstacles*

responsibilities who's suddenly and unexpectedly lost his job! But his fears about his future only made things worse.

The way to get him thinking more positively was to challenge his beliefs. The first step was to make Cal more aware of his reaction. I asked him, "Cal, if you were sitting in my chair looking and listening to you, what would you think?" He pondered the question. "I'd see a guy who was frightened and a bit panicky." I nodded in agreement.

I then asked, "Do you know of any other executive who's left your bank, and has landed a job?" Cal replied, "Yes, Dave is a friend of mine, a peer who actually lost his job last year due to a consolidation, and he is now a VP at a large credit union in town." He paused and smiled ever so slightly, "Yeah, Dave. That's encouraging."

As we continued our discussion, Cal revealed that his last job wasn't the perfect situation for him, didn't play to his strengths. He had previously worked in commercial lending, but the former SVP had asked him to take a short-term position in compliance. The compliance assignment ended up lasting three years.

He said his new boss, hired from the outside less than a year ago, was a bit of a jerk, and Cal believed his own career could grow no farther there.

As we talked about the hiring climate, he surmised the economy and job market had improved the past few years. He mentioned a former co-worker, now at a competitor, who was well-connected with executive search specialists and always seemed to know about the executive openings in town. He said he'd reach out to him.

As Cal summarized his eight years at the company, he had had some impressive accomplishments, was recognized and rewarded for his successes, and clearly had an overall positive story. He learned that a job that is not a good fit may work for a while, but eventually it will come to a head. He acknowledged he probably should have started an external search a year ago, when it was apparent he was not going to be moved out of Compliance any time soon.

I asked if he still saw the situation as dire as what he described when we began talking. He said, "No, it's not so bad. If I'm honest, I'd probably ridden that horse as far as it was going to take me. It was a good run. And they've given me a fair severance package. But you know, with new bosses, and a job that was not a great fit for me, that's a combination for change.

"I think reaching out to my network, and emphasizing my track record of success in the past in commercial lending, I should be able to find my way back into it."

Cal had changed his belief about his firing, and the consequences then changed, too. He assessed his situation more realistically. Now, he was better equipped to move forward in a constructive way.

#8: Forgiving Past Hurts

Unfortunately, everyone gets hurt or betrayed at one time or another. We all suffer injuries we don't deserve. How do we deal with this?

According to the late Lewis Smedes, a renowned thought leader on the topic of forgiveness, we have two options for responding to an undeserved wrong. One is vengeance – a passion for getting even. The problem is, you can never get even. And even if you cause your enemy the worst possible pain, it won't make you feel any better. Revenge brings no lasting joy.[19]

The other option is forgiveness. Smedes wrote that it has three stages. First, you rediscover the humanity of the person who hurt you. Secondly, you surrender your right to get even. Third, you revise your feelings toward the person: you forgive him.

When we forgive, we stop surrendering to the unfair pain of the past. Forgiveness doesn't mean a reunion. We can forgive with no strings attached. We can move on. It brings less stress and tension, more happiness.

Forgiving opens our future for better possibilities: to move past the negative emotions and reclaim our happiness. Watch these short videos[20] for more on how to raise your happiness through forgiveness[21]:

https://www.youtube.com/watch?v=8o9_TlZyB_Y

https://www.youtube.com/watch?v=EpclyrcMMHs

Forgiveness doesn't mean tolerating wrong, forgetting what happened, excusing the person who committed the wrong, dismissing the evil, nor surrendering our right to justice. It

---

[19] Lewis Smedes. *The Art of Forgiving: When you Need to Forgive and Don't Know How*

[20] The Science of Happiness video – *Forgive and Forget – The Phone Call* - SoulPancake

[21] The Science of Happiness video – *Forgive and Forget – SoulPancake*

certainly doesn't mean inviting the perpetrator to hurt you again.

"To forgive is to set a prisoner free and discover that the prisoner was you."

- Lewis Smedes

To summarize, you've learned eight Happiness Skills to help you become happier and sustain it.

Step 4:
Reclaim Your Energy, Then Time

Managing The Four Sources of Energy

Most of us expend massive amounts of time and effort on work. Our hypercompetitive, always-on culture seems to require longer work hours than ever. Few could be busier, or asked to do more. They're maxed out, often overwhelmed by requests, information, and distractions--and struggling to keep up. Not enough time to do it all.

As conscientious, hard workers, when we feel under pressure, we work longer and later. We push harder. We sacrifice our exercise time, sleep, social lives, and healthy, relaxing meals. And because of the law of diminishing returns, our output drops, in relation to our inputs.

We need a new way of working. It requires a self-assessment: an "off-site" with ourselves. We'll fly up to 35,000 feet, to get a bird's-eye view of how we're operating. Then we'll retool, to reinvent how we use our energy and time.

No matter who or what you blame for your workload, you are responsible for both the problem and finding the solution. Most people operate far below our potential. You're capable of much more than what you realize. You need to accept that time is finite; once expended, it cannot be regained. Energy, on the other hand, can be renewed, if you are more intentional about how you expend and renew your energy.

Your first job is to manage your energy. You control it, your attention, and your concentration; then you can leverage time. This will make you much more energized, effective, and happy.

In ***Be Excellent at Anything: The Four Keys to Transforming the Way We Work and Live,*** author Tony Schwartz identifies four sources of energy. Each influences the others; none is sufficient by itself. [22]

They are:

---

[22] Tony Schwartz. *Be Excellent at Anything: The Four Keys to Transform the Way We Work and Live*

Physical Energy.   Physical energy is your foundation, the energy you bring to life and work. To maintain it, sleep and exercise are the most important factors.

Studies show that 97% of people need 7-8 hours of sleep. Yet when you get behind the eight-ball at work, you might get up earlier, to compensate. When I ask groups of busy people, *"How much sleep do you get?"* one quarter say, less than 5 hours on average, one quarter say 5 to 6 hours, one quarter say 6 to 7 hours, less than a quarter say 7 to 8 hours--and very few say 8 hours or more.

These sleep-deprived folks are part of a bigger picture. The U.S Center for Disease Control estimates that more than 40 million American workers, 30% of the workforce, get less than six hours of sleep. In 2011, researchers at Harvard Medical School estimated that sleep deprivation costs American companies more than $63.2 billion per year in lost productivity. The lost opportunity costs must far exceed even that.

Sleep deprivation has a serious effect on the quality of your decisions, your mood, your happiness--and your health. Sadly, however, operating on little sleep has become a merit badge of sorts at many companies. The belief is: the less you sleep, the harder you work--and the more productive you are. This makes for an unhealthy, ultimately unsustainable situation. Making 80 hours per week of poor judgments is no way for you to operate!

Besides enough sleep, regular physical exercise is essential. Exercise has been shown to reduce more than half of anxiety symptoms. It improves how you process fear and anxiety: it is the best way to manage stress. If that's not enough, it also gives you a 20% energy boost.

Exercise is so powerful because it lifts us mentally and emotionally, acting like a vaccine, says the Journal of the American Medical Association.

Unfortunately, fewer than 15% of Americans engage in vigorous activity 20 minutes a day, three times a week. Some 25% are almost completely sedentary; 60% are only sporadically active.

In ***Become an Elite Mental Athlete: Commit to Building Your Brain and Improving Your Mental Game,*** author David Silverstein writes of "...strong correlations between effective leadership and regular exercise. Co-workers give higher leadership effectiveness ratings to executives who exercise, including in credibility, leading others and authenticity. Despite the findings, less than 50% of execs surveyed say they themselves are role models for diet, health and fitness. When asked about other senior leaders, just 33% said their colleagues were role models of healthfulness."[23]

Another study showed that fewer than 25% of workers feel their leaders model sustainable work practices. When they do, team members are 55% more engaged, 77% more satisfied at work, and 1.15 times more likely to stay at the company. And their trust in their leaders doubles.

Do you have the physical strength and stamina to tackle the opportunities that lie ahead? Do you feel ignited, eager to get going in the morning? Maintaining physical energy is partly about renewing yourself, by disengaging and resting.

But look at the bright side: most people have a big opportunity to better expend and renew their physical energy. Do you?

---

[23] David Silverstein. *Become an Elite Mental Athlete: Commit to Building Your Brain and Improving Your Mental Game*

Emotional Energy. If physical energy concerns quantity, emotional energy concerns quality. Emotional intelligence is the capacity to manage your emotions in a skillful way. It requires self-awareness, self-control, social awareness, and strong relationship capabilities.

Your emotional energy is best expended when you're guided by explicit, core, inviolable values. This allows you the confidence to take on challenges while showing compassion. It also makes it possible to include fun and enjoyment in your work.

Time for some reflection. Think about how you perform, when you're at your best. How would you describe that feeling? The emotions that you experience? Write them in your logbook.

With a demanding and hectic life, you may often not feel like you're performing at your best. But the good news is, you can develop that emotional "muscle," by becoming aware of how you feel, of your emotional energy--and renewing it. This not only makes you feel happier, but is a catalyst for greater productivity and performance in all key realms of life.

When you find yourself fatigued, disengaged, or burned out, what lifts you into a higher emotional state?

The fastest way is exercise. Taking a walk, going for a run, stretching, lifting weights, or using resistance bands is a great boost. Meditation can also be powerful for emotional renewal.

Mental energy. Mental energy is your ability to concentrate, to get your work done. Clarity, creativity, and thoughtful decision-making depend on it. Though the human brain represents less than 2% of body weight, it consumes 25% of your oxygen. Consequently, managing mental energy is critical for performance and engagement. If you can't concentrate, you can't collaborate and innovate. Too many people are feeling impatience, anxiety, and irritability at work.

The most successful people know it is impossible to concentrate 100% of the time at 100% capacity. So, they apply techniques to optimize their mental energy. They strive to minimize distractions.

The number of distractions that confront you these days, combined with the speed at which information comes your way, aggravates concentration problems. Multiple electronic devices bring you information constantly. You're likely pinged and notified and distracted till hell won't have it. It can feel as though you've given yourself ADHD. Trying hard to stay informed leads to becoming over-informed. And to manage all of this information leads you to multi-task.

But that's the wrong response. The single most effective approach to maintain your mental energy is to single-task--by, and while, eliminating distractions.

Spiritual Energy Spiritual energy is your commitment to inviolable values that you pursue in a purpose bigger than your own self-interest. It's about being congruent in your pursuit of a Purposeful Life. Do you have the courage to define and live by your values, even if it brings hardship and difficulty? At work, do you get to do what you do best?

When you lead with spiritual energy, you've defined your purpose--your North Star--and you have the courage and conviction to follow it. When you feel the work you do matters, you bring a greater level of commitment and energy to it. A deeply held faith can certainly renew your spiritual energy; it does so many. However, in the context we're describing spiritual energy, we aren't referring specifically to religion or faith, but to a purpose bigger than yourself.

Quit Running Marathons

A key is to view your workday as a series of sprints, with recovery periods built in--not a grueling marathon.

Sprinters can go full out, because they can see the finish line from the starting line. They know that, at the end of the race, they'll rest and recover.

Marathoners can't see the finish line until the very end of the race. Over their long run, it's easy to get distracted, and lose motivation. The vast majority of executives operate like they are running an ultra-marathon.

Engaging in concentrated, single-task, 60- to 90-minute periods of work sprints, followed by 10- to 15-minute breaks, is optimal. Leaders must show leadership in creating a sustainable way of working, then encouraging team members to do the same. It's the leader's responsibility to be the role model. How you manage energy is contagious – for better or worse.

Take control of their energy by finding a sustainable balance between expending and renewing. And by showing others how to do it, too. By doing this, you stay focused, engaged, and productive.

The Days that Got Away

Emily was the well-respected Managing Director of Chicago's largest annual show in the home landscaping business. Each year, she and her small team put on a multi-million-dollar, weeklong business-to-consumer show, with hundreds of exhibitors, tens of thousands of attendees. It is one of the most successful and largest shows her company runs.

She loves the creative aspects, and turning her exhibitors into friends who come back year after year to work with her and her team.

But when she described her typical workday, it was quite similar to what I hear from many other professionals.

Her alarm rang at 6 a.m. She'd take a few minutes to wake up and make small talk with her husband, Steve; flip on the local news; and get her teenage daughters up and ready for the bus to school--all while replying to emails in the kitchen. Her daughters and Steve grabbed a quick breakfast and left at 7:30. Out the door of her Evanston home by 7:45, with her third cup of coffee in her travel mug, she'd be on her way to client meetings and sales calls.

She tried to wrap all those up by noon, and head for her downtown Chicago office. Her assistant, Dianne, would order a sandwich or salad; she'd try to inhale it between 1 and 1:15 pm, when the afternoon round of meetings would begin.

As Emily averaged only about six hours of sleep a night, she'd start to fade by 3 p.m. So she'd take the elevator downstairs to the convenience store, ironically located on the 2nd floor, across from the building's fitness center. She'd get a Diet Coke -- or, more often than she'd like to admit, a candy bar or bag of chips for a quick energy boost. Feeling guilty about her choice of snacks, she'd promise herself that next week she'd start working out at the fitness center.

Client calls, email, and meetings kept her busy until 5:45 or so. Most evenings found her calling her husband to figure out who'd pick up dinner, or whip up something to eat -- assuming everyone would be home together. Then, she'd coordinate drop offs and pickups, or attend one of her daughters' sporting events, concerts, practices, or recitals. She'd do her best to help with homework, and have some family time, often while responding to email on her iPad, or taking a call from one of her sales reps.

After the girls retired to their rooms, Emily and Steve would share some wine and watch TV until midnight. Her iPad was just an arm's length away; she was always ready to respond to email from a colleague, or tackle some unfinished work. Emily knew she stayed up later than was ideal, but valued her time with Steve.

During the week, she rarely made time to catch up with extended family or friends, nor for gym or yoga. Emily felt constantly rushed, overscheduled and overstressed. She felt she was sacrificing her health and well-being to her job. She couldn't imagine maintaining this pace for the next two decades. Something had to give.

And this was her schedule during the "pre-season." In the two months leading up to her show, and the 10 days of it, she got even busier.

Emily regretted that she couldn't give her children and husband the consideration, time, and care they deserve. As the holidays drew near, with the show right around the corner, she got a knot in her stomach that stayed with her until it was over. She was unable to relax and enjoy the holidays. She felt she had the weight of the world on her shoulders. Even two weeks after the show closed each year, she confessed she was exhausted, frequently ill.

Emily knew something had to give--just not exactly what, or how to go about it. Reinvention was the key.

Because she was a perfectionist, Emily was not tapping the full commitment of her team. Like many talented professionals, who like things just so, she loaded herself up with the key responsibilities and made all important decisions, rather than delegating. Everything revolved around her, and her team members felt disengaged and disempowered. She sensed this, but her response was to take on even more. She operated as a super individual contributor. Instead of leading, she labored.

Can you relate to Emily's life? Sound familiar?

Her coach encouraged her to see herself as the show CEO, because successful CEOs are ruthless about how they spend their time. They don't do other people's jobs. They delegate.

She stopped her "hands-on" individual contributor approach, and implemented a more visionary and coaching style with her staff. She carefully managed her time, calendar, and priorities. She watched what she ate and drank. She made sure to go to bed by 11, and get at least seven hours sleep per weeknight, eight-nine on weekends.

Energy in Summary

The more effectively you manage your energy, and support others in managing theirs, the more likely you'll experience higher levels of happiness, productivity and success.

> "The world outside is getting more brutal every day. We focus on expanding personal energy from the inside to confront it."
>
> — Jim Loehr

Leveraging Your Time

To climb a tall mountain takes planning the route carefully and using time wisely. The possibility of suddenly changing weather, equipment failure, fatigue, and other unforeseen challenges makes deliberate, intentional planning essential. A climber couldn't afford to devote time, energy, or other resources to anything that wasn't a means to achieving his goal.

Leading a purposeful life, you must manage your time and energy with the same level of care—so as to build capacity to take on bigger, more challenging mountains.

This doesn't mean working harder or longer; as we've already discussed, most everyone is already working full out. The answer is to work differently. The following seven keys to leveraging time will bring you the biggest increase in productivity. Implementing them is a key step to time mastery.

1. Boosting Mood and Energy Level Mood has a dramatic effect on productivity. Operating optimally puts you in a good place mentally, concentrating on the task at hand. You are upbeat, engaged and optimistic, well-rested, well-nourished, and hydrated. Attending to mood and energy levels, and making any necessary adjustments before beginning a challenging project, is a pro's move.

As others take their emotional cues from you, your mood is contagious. Your number-one job is to be in a good mood – a positive emotional state.

As consistently as they can, high achievers take the first 90 minutes of the day to lay the groundwork for high productivity. A morning routine, with little variation, sets the stage for a positive mood.

2. Protecting from distractions. The greatest threat to higher productivity is information overload. Futurist Buckminster Fuller expressed the idea of the "Knowledge Doubling Curve." He concluded that, until 1900, human knowledge doubled every century. At the end of World War II, knowledge doubled approximately every 25 years. Now, according to IBM, the "internet of things" leads to the doubling of knowledge every 12 hours. There's more information than we can possible absorb. It flies at us on every PC, tablet, and smartphone we own.

All this makes us feel we must respond 24/7. And a host of other factors combine to create "weapons of mass distraction."

Weapons of Mass Distraction
- Email
- Text messages
- News alerts
- Social media
- Phone calls
- Knock at door
- Others

Our ability to adjust to all this has lagged behind—and always will. The result is a feeling of being overwhelmed: anxiety and stress.

To live your Purposeful Life means intentionally separating from your world from "the crazy world" at large. You turn off the devices that claim your time and attention, sucking precious time and creativity from what really matters. You especially avoid such distractions when your energy level is high. You avoid multi-tasking: one of the biggest productivity cripplers out there. Multi-tasking actually makes people dumber!

You can do a physical and mental activity simultaneously, like listening to a podcast or a book on audio while running on the treadmill. But the human brain can't efficiently combine two mental activities: for example, participating in a conference call while reading email.

This cripples your productivity. Multi-tasking is a myth. Try this: Out loud, count to 1-10 as fast as you can. Now the same, with the first 10 letters of the alphabet, A-J.

Now, combine the two: A1-J10, fast as you can. What happens? It takes longer, you're less accurate, and it's harder. It's actually not multi-tasking—it's task-switching, which causes work to slow down, and efficiency to drop.

If you need a reminder about the inefficiency of multitasking in the future, remember this.

A way to break the pattern is to commit not to multi-task for a week. That means devoting full attention to whatever single thing you're doing. This will reduce stress, improve your well-being and make you more productive.

3. Emphasizing Your Essentials. What are your vital few functions--and how much time do you spend on them? Most people, when introduced to this concept, admit it's a small percentage of their time. You need to drive that percentage higher and higher.

Steve Jobs, Apple's late CEO, reduced his vital three functions to one: launching revolutionary new products. He spent up to three hours a day on it. The iPod, then the iPhone, then the iPad. What are your vital three? What's your vital one? If Steve Jobs did it, what's your excuse for not doing it?

Once you've defined your vital functions, then what are your vital priorities? Forcing yourself to identify them prevents you from having too many choices. Jim Collins, author of ***Good to***

Great, writes, "If you have more than three priorities, you don't have any."[24]

To operate with three vital priorities means you'll have to learn to say "no" to all the invitations, intriguing projects, and other requests that don't advance your vital priorities. You keep yourself from doing what you shouldn't. When in doubt, say "No."

What are the Vital 3?

- Functions
- Goals

Look at your calendar for the last month. What should you have said "no" to? How about your calendar for tomorrow and the next week? What should you say "no" to?

In summary, the vital few concept is, concentrate on less, to accomplish more. Work on what is truly important: your three vital functions. Spend 90% of your time on them. Then you define the big priorities that move the business forward. You closely track their progress. And every day, you identify the most important task – the "Big Rock" – for each of them.

---

[24] Jim Collins. *Good to Great: Why Some Companies Make the Leap...And Others Don't*

Write those vital priorities and Big Rocks in your logbook. The act of constructing your goals in concrete terms, and writing them down, makes you 50% more likely to attain them, and 32% more likely to feel in control of your life. Each day, what are the three Big Rocks you need to move for progress to be made on your vital few priorities?

4. Stopping, starting, continuing You think carefully about how to approach your job, and allocate your time. Review your calendar and "to-do" lists for the past several months. Ask yourself, "Where have I spent my time?" Most of us can allocate five "big buckets" that eat up 90% of our time: for example, meetings with customers and team, sales calls, email, phone calls, reviewing reports, responding to requests from the boss, administrative tasks.

So, historically reflecting on your top five "buckets," ask yourself:

- What have I produced?

- What's been the main thrust of my efforts?

- What is the first thing I've done each day?

- Who have I met with?

- When I've been tied up, what type of work have I returned to first?

Given how you've been spending your time, and now considering your newly defined vital functions, vital priorities and Big Rocks, what do you need to stop doing?

"We spend a lot of time teaching leaders what to do. We don't spend enough time teaching leaders what to stop. Half the leaders I have met don't need to learn what to do. They need to learn what to stop."

— Peter Drucker

Saying "No" and stopping is critical to increasing your productivity. Identify and list at least 10 practices, meetings, reports, activities, habits, etc., you must stop doing. You delegate these responsibilities to someone else, outsource them, automate them, or do without them altogether. They are lower-value activities.

Also--what must you start? What very few, new initiatives should you launch? They should be high-value activities that have the potential to create big gains in improvement and growth.

Finally, what activities should you continue?

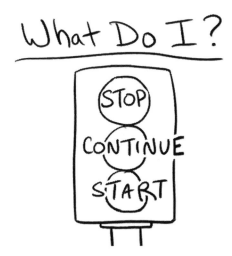

Every three to four months, considering your vital few functions, priorities and Big Rocks, reviewing how you allocate your time, and identifying what you must stop, start, and continue, is a powerful tool to reinvent your leadership, stay energized, and create great value. Right now, pick 10 things to stop – list them in your logbook and promise yourself within the next two days, you'll put in place the plan to discontinue those lower value activities.

5. Running Sprints, not Marathons

Reinventors living a Purposeful Life break the marathon paradigm for themselves. They know the key to greater productivity and higher performance is to think of the day as a series of sprints. They see each nearby finish line, and go all-out to reach it, knowing they'll have time to rest and renew before the next sprint.

In business and creative work, using the sprinter's approach leads to greater productivity. Elite world-class performers apply the sprinter's approach: concert violinists, Olympic athletes, entertainers. Here's how:

As they schedule their day, they book two or three 60-90 minute blocks of "sprint" time. During these blocks, they concentrate on the task at hand--and produce. The concert pianist practices his score deliberately, for a set time. Similarly, you create a bubble of silence, so he can do intentional, concentrated work.

First, you clear the deck. Set the timer on your smartphone for 60, 75 or 90 minutes—then, turn off the ringer. You work on the most important task until it's done, or the alarm rings.

Then, you take 10 to 15 minutes to recharge: go for a walk, listen to music, do some light exercise, meditate, or grab a healthy snack. That prepares you for whatever comes next. Expend energy then renew, rejuvenate.

Back to Emily: During the workday, she developed a routine, and followed it carefully. She ate more frequent, smaller, healthier meals. She scheduled uninterrupted Sprint 1 from 7:45 to 9, to tackle the biggest challenge of the day. At 11, she ate a healthful snack. After morning calls, she got to the office at 1. Lunch consisted of a protein smoothie or salad.

From 2 to 3:30, she attended internal meetings and handled other work. From 3:30 – 3:45, she "recharged" with a snack, meditation, or soft music.

Sprint 2 was from 3:45 – 5. It involved one-on-ones with staff or client calls, and allowed for a short break. Sprint 3 came from 5 to 5:45: time for calls, emails, planning for the next day, and writing in her logbook.

By planning her time carefully, Emily found her productivity rising and she was eventually able to squeeze in an hour at the club, to exercise, four days a week.

Emily scheduled her evenings just as carefully. Family time came from 6:30 to 8:30. After a quick check of her email, no more than 15 minutes, she spent the rest of her waking time with her husband.

All of this brought Emily better control at home, better performance at work, a more engaged staff—a happier, healthier life. It gave her new perspective. She no longer felt that the whole show depended on her, and grew better able to handle "curveballs" that life pitched her way.

The following year, Emily experienced the show in a vastly different way. She had reinvented how she presents herself and operates. She lived with purpose. She was happy.

6. Scheduling Your Greatness Everyone has a "to-do" list, but it's useless – unless you book time for your three vital priorities and Big Rocks on your calendar. This forces you to confront the most important "must-do's," reducing the urge to procrastinate and lose concentration. It helps you become more efficient. It empowers you to say "no" to what you shouldn't or needn't be doing.

You schedule quitting time first, and work backwards from there. You schedule at least two daily sprints. A look at your calendar, how you spend your time, shows your real priorities.

This works for free time and training time, too. Those who control their calendars, and stay mindful about investments in time, stay energized. Losing control of your calendar leads to burnout. Controlling your calendar give you the time to focus on your greatness. Living the purposeful life and unveiling the masterpiece that lies within.

7. Implementing a Rock-Solid Routine Each day, you work your reinvention plan —and stay on course. How? By creating and living by a rock-solid daily routine. World-class athletes and performers do this, too.

A routine gives you the necessary structure, becomes your framework for happiness, inspiration and production. It forms your personal work system. No matter how busy you are, you can almost always bookend the day: control the first and last hours, even if the middle of the day takes unexpected turns. You also set a bedtime to get enough sleep, and a time to awaken. High achievers wake early, so they go to bed earlier too.

You self-consciously follow a routine until it becomes habitual. Then, it no longer takes willpower. Willpower is tough to rely on; research shows it can be relied on only three to four times a day. Creating habits is easier and works better.

Your early-morning routine, before you go to work, should vary as little as possible. It leads to a calm, mindful state. You can use it for exercise, reflection, prayer, and a healthy breakfast. Ideally, you run your first 60-90 minute sprint at home.

Each evening, you identify your most important goals for the following day. What steps do you need to take to accomplish your vital few – your Big Rock goals? You'll concentrate on them in your first sprint.

Another habit you develop is daily journaling: using your logbook. Acknowledging you probably don't have much time to journal, commit to a 10-minute daily "speed" journal, at the end of the day, reflecting on five questions:

- What's the best thing that happened today?

- What must go better tomorrow?

- What are the Big Rocks I moved today?

- What the Big Rocks must I concentrate on tomorrow?

- What am I grateful for?

Journaling allows you to close out the day and plan for tomorrow. Especially concentrate on the last question, "What am I grateful for?" Showing gratitude for the good things in life is the most powerful happy boosting activity there is. That will lift your spirits, make you a better person. So especially in periods where you are really feeling the pressure to deliver, writing about two or three people or things you are grateful for - daily - is important for keeping your perspective and in a positive mood.

Don't let yourself off the hook on your 10-minute speed journaling. If you haven't found time earlier in the day, complete it before you turn in for the night. Writing down your responses will allow you to sleep better. You won't have to worry about forgetting your plan for the next day.

Finally, you create a routine for a weekly review. Many like to do it 15-30 minutes Sunday nights, and plan the upcoming week. It's a perfect way to kill Sunday-night dread. Review your logbook, and the previous week's activities. When you see you've made progress on your priorities, it raises your satisfaction and commitment to reinvention.

Reinventing means harnessing and aligning physical, mental, emotional, and spiritual energy, to achieve top performance—and serve the world. This means claiming your power and taking control of time. Rock-solid morning and evening routines pulls it together.

Step 5:
Reinvent by Training, not just Trying

You've made it to Step 5, and you are closing in on the finish line! Congratulations.

As you've seen, there is no shortage of ideas on how to reinvent yourself – to reinvent your happiness - so you can flourish. You've learned the steps to define a Purposeful Life for yourself. You've discovered eight happiness skills, how to reinvigorate your relationships, ways to create greater energy, and tools to carve out more time, so you can do what makes you happy. All good stuff.

Now, it's time to put together a happiness reinvention "game plan," so you can create happiness every day. At this point, you've got everything you need to reinvent and be happier. But that information is useless if you don't put it into action and make it a part of your routine. It's time to build a plan to do your happiness work.

The goal of this section is to persuade you to put your plan together and inspire you to implement it. You achieve happiness not by trying for it—but by training for it. Those are two very different things. Trying requires only interest. Training requires deep commitment. Repeaters try. Reinventors train.

"There isn't anything that isn't made easier through familiarity and training. Through training, we can transform ourselves."
— Dalai Lama

To live purposefully, to achieve happiness, to make change stick, to live happily and flourish, requires discipline. Sorry, no short cuts. In preparing your plan, think of yourself as a world-class performer or a highly trained athlete. To reach and sustain elite-level performance, you must engage in deeply committed practice – what Doug Lemov, author of **Practice Perfect: 42 Rules for Getting Better at Getting Better,** calls "getting better at getting better." [25]

Legendary college football coach Paul "Bear" Bryant once said, "It's not the will to win that matters—everyone has that. It's the will to prepare to win that matters." If you're going to win at what you do, you have to prepare. And that means shifting your mindset from trying to training.

---

[25] Doug Lemov. *Practice Perfect: 42 Rules for Getting Better at Getting Better*

Don't Fall Victim to the New Year's Syndrome

Each year, 87% of adults in the USA create New Year's resolutions-- more than 200 million people. But the vast majority experience the same frustrating results: false starts, empty promises, and failure. Consider:

- 25% abandon their resolutions within one week;

- 50% abandon their resolutions within one month;

- The average person makes the same resolutions 10 times without success.

Change is difficult. Resolutions don't work. But reinvention does, if you go about it the right way. Breakthroughs are possible in every part of life. To make positive change stick will take a reinvention process that connects with your deepest motivations, shows you how to create a future vision of success, establishes breakthrough goals for the parts of life most in need of change, and overcomes the inevitable obstacles and barriers that seek to derail you. To keep your reinvention efforts front-and-center, you need a rock-solid daily routine. You need to envision a fabulous 2016. And you need to train, to make that happen.

A Better Solution than Brute Force

Training means doing what you need, to accomplish what you cannot by simple effort: by just trying.

If you're asked something you don't know how to do, or are unable to do, trying will not be enough. You can try brute force, but we know that's not sustainable. Training is essential. It provides the path. It not only gives you the ability to perform, but raises your proficiency. It makes you better.

Do you overestimate what you can do by trying, and underestimate what you can do by training? Probably, if you are like most people.

You might try very hard to win the Boston Marathon. But if you've not trained, you won't finish--never mind win. Without training, your muscles let you down, sooner or later. As little as a couple of days before the race, no amount of cramming will help make up for failure to train.

When you try, you don't have to plan or prepare. But you keep "trying" only as long as your interest is piqued. To meet your goals, you've got to plan--then train.

Not building in time to train, not engaging in deliberate, intentional practice, is a mistake. Those who fail to train are most vulnerable to being disrupted--to be moved aside, or out.

As you've read this book, and journaled in your logbook, you've had time to reflect. What's been your experience with training? Are you training now? In what parts of your life and work do you need more training? How should you deepen your skills, to become your best as a person?

Let's go back to the Wheel of Happiness, the eight key parts of life. Review your score for each of the eight key parts:

- Spirit
- Health and Fitness
- Family
- Significant Other
- Career
- Finances
- Friends

- Fun

Now on a scale of 1 to 10, what is the current level of importance in each key part of life, and what is the energy level you're spending on each? For each, considering your current level of happiness, the level of importance, and the energy level you're investing, where must you make changes?

In the Reinventing Your Energy, then Time section, you learned techniques to be more productive. I suggested that you implement daily "sprints" and at least 10 "stops": tasks you decided to discontinue, because they weren't worth your time. You've improved your physical energy, and greatly reduced interruptions and distractions. You have additional capacity now.

"It wasn't raining when Noah built the ark."

-Howard Ruff

Now, concentrate on your training. Commit to deliberate, intentional practice and training to become your best.

Create a Happiness Reinvention Game Plan

Training begins with making a Happiness Reinvention Game Plan. For it to work, it needs two elements:

First, leverage the 20/80 rule. What one skill and one habit will make a huge difference for your happiness in the near term? It forms the basis of your training plan. Maybe it's a plan to...

- Strengthen your relationship with your significant other.

- Have family dinner together at least three times a week.

- Get on a sensible diet and exercise plan and drop 15 pounds, once and for all.

- Recommit to and strengthen your faith and spiritual life.

- Start a new business that aligns with your Purposeful Life.

- Find a small group of other like-minded men or women.

- Discover how to create and tell the essential stories that every leader needs to tell, to inspire others.

Second, set a specific objective. To run on a treadmill for 40 minutes a day is a task. But preparing to run a 10k race in 40 minutes or less is a *goal*, which gives you intensity. How will you "objectify" your training, to get a better return on your investment of time and energy? How will you know you are making progress toward your goal?

To make your reinvention a reality, you'll need to set and achieve breakthrough goals. What are they? Get started!

a. Write them down. Make them explicit and specific. For each key part of life. Research shows that written goals are 42% more likely to be achieved.

b. Make them exciting. For instance, one of my goals under the Family and Fun parts is to take a seven-day trip this July with my son and grandsons, visiting several cities to see Major League Baseball games. We're mapping out a plan starting in Minneapolis, then Chicago, then Milwaukee, then back to Chicago—six games in all, with one day at an amusement and water park. This is a goal that grabs my heart, excites me.

c. Dedicate each goal to someone. That strengthens your motivation. Maybe it's for someone you love. When you connect a goal with someone you love, you're more likely to achieve it. For instance, in dedicating that baseball vacation trip to my son and grandsons, I'm committed to seeing it through. I won't let work or other priorities interfere. It's a far stronger commitment than if I considered only my own enjoyment. For whom can you dedicate each of your goals?

d. Identify one big catalyst goal. A catalyst goal is one that when achieved, explodes into the other goals. It acts like a domino. It's the 20% that gets the other 80%. For example, if you are self-employed, and land a huge client deal early in the year, that might be a catalyst goal, improving your career, finances, and perhaps other parts. Or, if you dropped 25 pounds to improve your cardiovascular fitness, that might also be a catalyst for better satisfaction with family and significant other, and more fun. What's your catalyst goal?

e. Break down your breakthrough goals. Breakthrough goals may seem as high as a mountain when created. Maybe too much of a stretch. To begin and sustain progress, break them down into achievable weekly and daily steps. Over time, with the cumulative effect in place, progress towards your goal mounts, and eventually, great things can be accomplished.

f. Review your breakthrough goals weekly. A weekly review of progress toward your goals is critical. Celebrate your wins. Make adjustments where you've fallen short. Remember that you want to keep momentum. Don't beat yourself up if you fall a bit short one week; that will happen. Adjust as necessary, and keep moving forward. Progress, not perfection, is your aim. Perfection is the enemy of progress, so keep taking one step forward at a time.

Mindfulness and Meditation

It's been reported more than 60,000 thoughts run through our heads each day. That's a staggering, overwhelming number. To step away from them, to quiet your mind, you need to practice mindfulness, and gain clarity, harness creativity, relieve stress, and boost your energy. To be mindful is to look inward and observe, without judgment. Journaling, long walks, prayer, and introspection are all powerful mindfulness practices.

Meditation is another, free and easy to learn. It has been shown to work better than medication. You can practice it in almost anywhere—in your office, at home, or on a plane. It's a perishable skill that you'll want to practice daily. The more often you do it, the better the outcomes. When you do, you'll quiet your thoughts, train yourself to concentrate, and relax. It's like a reboot for you.

Meditation has gone mainstream. Bill George, former CEO of Medtronic; Andrew Cherng, founder of Panda Express; Marc Benioff, founder and CEO of salesforce.com; Roger Berkowitz, CEO of Legal Sea Foods; and Oprah Winfrey are high-powered leaders who meditate daily. Such companies as Google, Apple, Goldman Sachs, and General Mills see its benefits, and offer classes and meditation rooms to their staffs.

You don't need instruction to meditate. The more books I read about it, in an attempt to find new ways to master the art, the more it becomes like work--which is want I need a break from! And, the more complicated you make it, the more likely you'll go for months without doing it – and then, pay the price.

Yet meditation can be very simple. For example, here's a simple technique: Just shut your eyes and count your breaths. Count on the inhale, concentrate on the number of each long breath, and exhale for a little longer than you inhale. Keep it comfortable. You don't need to sit in a lotus position or do anything else, if that's not comfortable.

If you find your mind wandering, liken the interruption to the waves of an ocean. The wave goes in; the wave goes out. Let the interruption come in, then go out. Return your attention to counting each deep breath. If you're worried you'll fall asleep, set the timer on your smart phone.

You say you don't have enough time? Everyone has time to shut their eyes and take 10 breaths. Time it. It takes about 90-100 seconds—but even so, it makes a difference. What if you increased to 100 breaths? That will take 13-15 minutes. How will you feel? Rejuvenated and renewed, for certain. Try it.

With the fast-paced life you likely lead, mindfulness is a must to stay balanced. Meditation is the essential training practice in every Reinventor's routine.

Back to Your Rock-Solid Routine

The Energy, then Time section introduced the rock-solid routine. It bears repeating, in the context of training. Bookend your day. Keep the first 60-90 minutes as consistent as you can. Take advantage of the last hour to reflect and journal. Build in time for training. Make it a habit, so you don't have to rely on willpower.

Organize your day for happiness and success. We say happiness is most important but fail to schedule in our calendars. Things that make you happy should be a habit, part of your routine, scheduled in to your calendar: a "happiness subscription"

Every Sunday, review, to track your progress. Make adjustments as necessary to stay on track. Celebrate your wins. Journal in your logbook. Challenge yourself to get better and better. Keep raising the bar.

To sum up: Reinventors undertake deliberate, intentional training. They train, not try. You know you must. Knowledge is important, but it alone won't bring change for the better. Training will, though--starting today!

"You will never change your life until you change something you do daily. The secret of your success is found in your daily routine." John C. Maxwell

"We are what we repeatedly do. Excellence, then, is not an act, but a habit."

- Aristotle

Pulling it All Together

The most important year in your happiness reinvention is this one. Let's create a clear vision of happiness and success for the next twelve months.

Time Magazine Person of the Year

You've defined your "Why." Now, it's time to move to your vision: a dream of an ideal future. What's does an ideal 2016 look like for you?

Vincent Van Gogh once told a friend, *"I dream my painting, and then I paint my dreams."* With your dream or vision in place, you can begin "painting" your year, just like Van Gogh painted his dreams.

To begin creating your vision for a glorious 2017, pull out your logbook. If relaxing classical music or smooth jazz helps you reflect, turn it on. Take a few deep breaths to calm your mind and body.

Now that you're in a reflective state, imagine it's late December 2017, and that 2017 has been a great year for you. There have been some ups and downs, but you've made excellent progress in the key parts of life. You've reinvented where you've needed to. You feel happy, confident, inspired, and justifiably proud of your great progress. You've noticed an enormous difference, and others around you have, too. So much that Time Magazine has selected you as *Person of the Year* for 2017, and the article about you runs as the cover story for their December 31, 2017, issue. Your job is to write the article, without any limiting beliefs. Let your every desire become reality. Start by capturing the themes for each key part of life.

Specifically, address the following:

- What does the article say about you?

- Reviewing each key part in the Wheel of Happiness, what has worked well for you in the past? What do you need to do differently?

- What was on your "to do" list? What was on your "to be" list?

- What old limiting beliefs did you let go of? What new empowering beliefs did you adopt?

- What five activities did you stop?

- How did you strengthen your relationships with the people you most love?

- Who did you meet for the first time?

- What are the emotions you wanted others to experience, when they rubbed shoulders with you?

- In what one part did you receive more training? What behavior did you change? What new skill did you develop? What new habit did you adopt?

- What did your daily routine look like?

- What were your greatest accomplishments?

- What were the biggest breakthroughs?

- What is your next big opportunity? How are you preparing for it?

Get going on your *Person of the Year* article. Make an outline with the themes of the article in each key part of life. Reflect on the questions above. Then, start writing your article in your logbook. Don't worry about grammar, spelling or punctuation. Set the alarm on your phone for 45 minutes, and start writing. Then read it over, and revise it as necessary. Use this 2016 vision to create the life to which you aspire.

Your One Word!

hat's the one word that can capture who you are trying to be and do for the next 12 months?

What's Your # 1 Word for the Year?

When you settle on it, write it in your journal! Tape it on your mirror, so you see it when you brush your teeth, and on the screen of your laptop. Make it the screen saver for your tablet and smartphone. Remind yourself constantly of it. Think about it. Meditate on it. Pray on it--especially when you face resistance.

Remember, two voices live within us. One is the Repeater, the amateur, the one who is satisfied with only the Pleasant Life, who does things the same way he's always done, or makes just small, incremental changes. The other is the Reinventor: the individual who lives the Good and Purposeful Life, who takes ownership of his happiness, who reinvents, who consciously transforms how he operates and connects, so he stays happy, energized and successful. He leads and lives on a higher plane, and serves a higher purpose.

Which do you listen to? Since you've read this far, you've decided to leave the Repeater behind—to become happier, most successful and become your best. You aspire to being a Reinventor in all ways.

Overcome the Inevitable Resistance

Yet you still have a battle to fight: the battle against resistance. Resistance is a most powerful force. It is invested in the status quo, and will work tirelessly to sabotage your efforts. Your ego relies on it, to keep you from becoming the person you aspire to become. Human nature fights like hell to prevent change. Resistance tries to prevent you from achieving your goals and grandest vision of yourself. It's insidious, and it can plague you forever. Resistance is fine with you pursuing only the Pleasant Life, trying to chase happiness in an unsustainable way.

Its weapons are formidable. It may strip you of your motivation. It may delude you into thinking you can't create greater happiness—that what has happened in the past will continue indefinitely. It will try to persuade you that reinvention is too hard, takes too long. Or maybe you'll try it halfheartedly, lose your enthusiasm, then claim it just doesn't work. It will encourage you to procrastinate. And it can derail you in many other ways: through negative self-talk, addictions, cynicism, distractions, fear of failure-- or even fear of success.

What will be your excuses? List them in your logbook. If you let them get in your way, you'll face the same limitations you always have. Don't surrender your power.

How do you overcome resistance? By believing in the deepest way possible, with every fiber of your body, in your "why," and the vision of your Purposeful Life. Committing to the flourishing person you seek to become. And by creating and living by a routine that overwhelms resistance.

It takes self-discipline. Resistance hates routine, structure, and concentration. Reinvention requires skill and will. Now you know the skill. It's up to you to muster the will. Reinventing your happiness and success is mostly will. Have the courage to do this, to do more and be more. Be unstoppable.

> Which pain will you choose? The pain of discipline or the pain of regret?
>
> – Jim Rohn

Reinvention is forever, an on-going process. It's never done. And when you follow the five critical steps, it is impossible for resistance to sabotage you.

It's Not Just For You

Your potential and promise is unknowable. It's not just for you. It's so that you can:

- Live a life of purpose.

- Inspire and lift others.

- Serve a great cause.

- Make a happy and meaningful impact on the world.

When you reinvent and live a Purposeful Life, you create a ripple that affects others. Who knows how many will benefit by that ripple? Tens, hundreds, thousands, more? So that when you reinvent your happiness and thrive, we all thrive. You give a gift that lasts forever. If you don't reinvent, everyone misses out on the gift you were made to give.

"What will you do with your life that will last forever?"

- Bill Hybels

It's Your Time for Happiness

Now, it's your time to reinvent. Don't settle for "couldas, wouldas, shouldas." Don't let excuses be your legacy. You have the knowledge. You know what to do. Kill the resistance. Get moving.

Change will occur, with or without you. Take control and reinvent your happiness, future and success. It's your birthright to be your best! This is your moment to shine.

Follow the steps, do the happiness work, maintain your unshakeable will and you are on your way to a Purposeful Life. If you fall down, pick yourself up and get going again. Keep moving forward.

To fulfill your promise and potential. To achieve your dreams. To live your life like you dream. To your well-being and happiness.

I admire and applaud you for your courage to reinvent your happiness. I look forward to hearing your story of happiness, reinvention and transformation. May this be the best and happiest year ever for you. All the best to you!

chuck@theboltongroup.com

Appendix 1:
The State of Our
Happiness in 2017

THE STATE OF OUR
HAPPINESS IN 2017:
WHAT WE'VE DISCOVERED

Assessment Background

- **The Happiness Report** self-assessment measures happiness in 8 key areas of life on a scale of 1 (low) to 10 (high). Scores are converted into percentiles. A customized happiness report is then created.

Assessment Demographics

- 1,461 people took the assessment at TheHappinessReport.com during 2016

Assessment Takers:
Baby Boomers by Gender

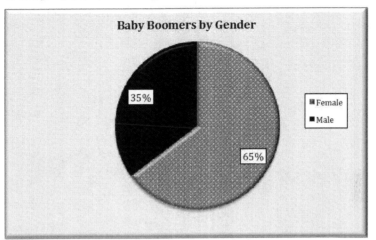

Assessment Takers:
Gen X by Gender

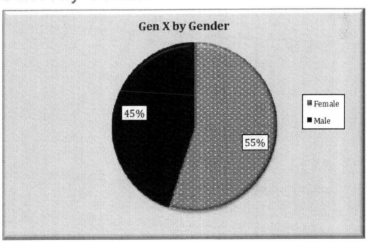

Assessment Takers: Millennials by Gender

Who's Happiest?

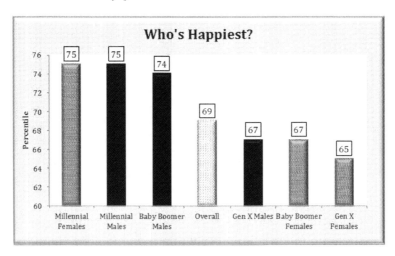

Happiness Level - Summary

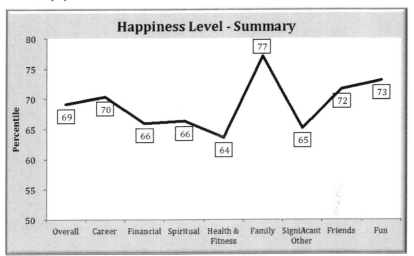

Assessment Results
By Gender

Assessment Results by
Gender for Baby Boomers

Assessment Results by
Gender for Millennials

Assessment Results
By Generation

Assessment Results for Females
by Generation

Assessment Results for Males by Generation

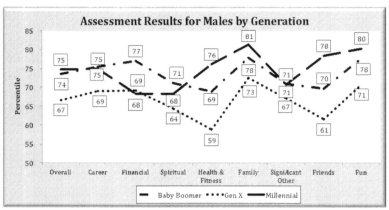

The State of Our
Happiness – Gaps by Gender

Baby Boomers

- Biggest happiness "gaps" between Baby Boomer Females and Males are:
  - Significant Other (14.8% points);
  - Financial (12.2% points);
  - Career (8.7% points);
  - Health/Fitness (7.9% points) and Fun (7.9% points)

The State of Our
Happiness – Gaps by Gender

<u>Gen X</u>

- Biggest happiness "gaps" between Gen X Females and Males are:
  - Financial (7.4% points);
  - Significant Other (6.9% points);
  - Friends (6.8% points);
  - Health/Fitness (6.2% points)

The State of Our
Happiness – Gaps by Gender

· <u>Millennials</u>
- Biggest happiness "gaps" between Millennial Females and Males are:
  - Financial (5.2% points);
  - Friends (3.0% points);
  - Significant Other (2.8% points);
  - Health/Fitness (2.3% points)

Most Happy / Least Happy

	Most Happy About	Least Happy About
Overall	Family (77), Fun (73)	Health/Fitness (64), Significant Other (65)
Females	Family (78), Friends (73)	Health/Fitness (62), Financial (63); Significant Other (63)
Males	Family (76), Fun (75)	Health/Fitness (67), Spirit (67)
Baby Boomer	Family (77), Fun (73)	Significant Other (62), Health/Fitness (64)
Baby Boomer - Female	Family (77), Friends (71)	Significant Other (56), Health/Fitness (61)
Baby Boomer - Male	Family (78), Fun (78)	Health/Fitness (69), Friends (70)
Gen X	Family (73), Fun (69)	Health/Fitness (55), Significant Other (63)
Gen X - Female	Family (74), Friends & Fun (68)	Health/Fitness (53), Significant Other (60)
Gen X - Male	Family (73), Fun (71)	Health/Fitness (59), Friends (61)
Millennials	Family (83), Friends & Fun (80)	Financial (65), Spiritual (70)
Millennials - Female	Family (83), Friends (81)	Financial (65), Spiritual (71)
Millennials - Male	Family (81), Fun (80)	Spiritual (68), Financial (69)

Next Steps

- 1.) Take the free *__The Happiness Report__* assessment to assess your current level of happiness and receive your customized report.
- 2.) Purchase *__Reinvent Your Happiness: Five Steps to Your Best Self__* at Amazon. Read the book and follow the steps.
- 3.) Complete the *__Happiness Reinvention Game Plan__* and commit to a plan of action to make 2017 a happy and successful year for you.
- 4.) Ask your significant other to also take *__The Happiness Report__* so you can partake in the happiness journey together.
- 5.) In three to six months, take *__The Happiness Report__* again to measure your progress.

Appendix 2:
More Tips to Increase Your Happiness in the Key Areas of Life

1. Significant Other

From **The Happiness Report**: On a scale of 1 (low) to 10 (high), please rate your level of agreement for each of the following statements.

- My partner or spouse and I have a healthy, thriving and loving relationship.

- My partner or spouse would agree I invest the time and energy to strengthen and deepen our relationship.

- When I am with my partner or spouse, I am totally focused and present in the moment with them.

Ideas to Boost:

- Give your significant other a kiss. Those who do live 5 yeas longer and make 20-30% more money.

Source: <u>Eric Barker 7 Ways Morning Ritual</u>

11 Ways to Make Your Long-term Marriage Happier Starting Today

1. Remind your partner (and yourself) that you appreciate them.

- Studies show that nearly half of men who have cheated say it was because of emotional dissatisfaction - and not sex. When men don't feel connected or appreciated by their wives, they are vulnerable to the advances of any attractive woman who casts a lustful glance in their way.

2. Say thank you for the little things. Don't keep score or play tit for tat.

3. Practice honesty, even when you are ashamed. While infidelity usually happens in bed, it can also happen with money.

4. Take care of your appearance

5. Foster relationships outside your marriage. Katie Couric asked Barbra Streisand and James Brolin the secret to their happy marriage, she replied, "time apart." Your marriage should be your primary relationship but it needn't be the only one.

6. Watch your words.

7. Put away the jumper cables yourself. The big things. The little things, the small annoyances that, if left unaddressed, do us in.

8. Relish the silence. Bite your tongue until the tip bleeds. And once in a while, remind yourself of why you married this person. Beatles, "Let it be."

9. Recognize the Ebb-and-Flow. Relationships aren't flat-lined. Life has ups and downs, peaks and valleys. You don't stay in either place forever. In marriage, you spend most of your time in an emotional middle ground.

10. Be Kind. "What can I do today to make my partner happy?"

11. Maintain intimacy and passion, both inside and outside the bedroom. And intimacy comes in many shapes, including conversation and cuddling.

Source:

http://www.huffingtonpost.com/2014/03/11/marriage-advice_n_4823414.html

What's the key to a happy relationship?

1. Practice self-love first.

- Make a list or mental note of all the things to appreciate about you. Everyone has flaws and there is a lot more right with you than wrong with you.

- Work on forgiving yourself. The past is the past and you deserve to put it behind you, but no one else can let it go for you.

- Be good to yourself today. Yoga, meditate, walk.

2. Focus on compatibility.

- Be best friends first.

- If you're single, do something you love to meet compatible people and foster your interests.

- In a relationship, spend some time sharing something you both enjoy.

3. Practice acceptance

- Accept that not everyone or everting is perfect. We're all perfectly flawed.

4. Have realistic expectations.

- If you feel yourself focusing on everything someone appears to be doing wrong, ask yourself if there's something else upsetting you. It's easier to blame others than it is to look in ourselves, but oftentimes that's where the problem is.

- Notice when you're projecting something onto the other person that has nothing to do with them, like fear from a past relationship. Then make an effort to let it go.

5. Be kind in words and deeds

- Think about the person's feelings before you speak or criticize them.

- Make an effort to really listen, not just wait to talk.

- See the other person as if for the first time. It's too easy to take someone for granted. Really notice all the wonderful things they do and let them know what you see.

6. Be honest

- If something is on your mind, express it without implying the other person is responsible for your feelings.

7. Remember to act.

- Have rich individual pursuits and pursue things together.

- Take time to laugh together, whether it is watching funny videos or trying something new together.

- It's a new day - a new chance to practice giving and receiving love.

Source:

http://tinybuddha.com/blog/7-vital-choices-for-happy-relationships/

Remind her why you were the best choice she's ever made.

- Introduce her with a compliment, "I'd like you to meet my beautiful wife."

- Ask how you can lift her burden. Being in tune with her needs emotionally and spiritually.

- Forgive her fast. With all she does right, let it go when she makes mistakes.

- Write her love letters. Focus on the specific things you love about her. How she's so cheery when you call her. How her dimple shows when she smiles that gorgeous, sexy smile.

Source:

https://familyshare.com/109/10-simple-ways-to-make-your-wife-happy

2. Family

From **_The Happiness Report_**: On a scale of 1 (low) to 10 (high), please rate your level of agreement for each of the following statements.

- I experience close, loving relationships with my immediate family members and/or good friends.

- I create opportunities for shared experiences and times with extended family members and/or good friends.

- When I am with family and/or good friends, I am totally focused and present in the moment with them

Ideas to Boost:

From 15 Secrets to Have a Happy Family

Use the 90 second rule. Swap stories. When home, kids have to come first.

Put marriage first.

Family dinners are essential. A minimum of four dinners per week.

Families need rituals. Bring family members closer together because they are repeated over time. Pizza night. Movie and popcorn night.

Source:

http://www.webmd.com/parenting/features/15-secrets-to-have-a-happy-family#1

The amount of time children spent eating meals at home was the single biggest predictor of better academic achievement and fewer behavioral problems.

Share the family history. The more children knew about their family's history, the stronger their sense of control over their lives, the higher their self-esteem, and the more successfully they believed their families functioned.

Kids who know this have a strong "intergenerational self." They know they belong to something bigger than themselves.

Children asked, "If you were granted one wish about your parents, what would it be?" The kids' number one wish was that their parents were less tired and less stressed.

Be part of a larger community. What matters is the number of friends you have in your religious community. Ten is the magic number; if you have that many, you'll be happier.

Religious people, are happier because they feel connected to a community of like-minded people.

Tap into grandma. With a grandma providing support, moms are less stressed.

Source:

http://time.com/21296/how-to-have-a-happy-family-7-tips-backed-by-research/

Create cuddle time. Cook together. Sing together and stay together. Read and write time together. Important for children to spend some time writing each day. Have routines. Prioritize the marriage.

Source:

http://www.rd.com/advice/parenting/13-tips-to-increase-your-familys-happiness-and-health/

3. Friends

From **The Happiness Report**: On a scale of 1 (low) to 10 (high), please rate your level of agreement for each of the following statements.

- I have two to three close friends (outside of significant other or family) with whom I can speak about anything on my head or heart.

- I have a small group of individuals with whom I meet regularly to talk, listen and encourage one another.

- I have a best friend.

Ideas to Boost:

1. They reduce your stress when times are tough. Being with a best friend during a stressful time reduce levels of the stress hormone cortisol, according to a 2011 study published in Developmental Psychology. People in the study didn't feel as upset about the experience if their best friend was around.

2. Being there for them cheers you up, too Sending a card, getting a bottle of wine when they've been under the guy makes you *both* feel better.

3. Even casual friends boost your mood. People at spin class, or folks at church.

4. The good feeling of a friendship lasts and lasts. Not like the hedonic adaptation of getting a new house or car. So, keep scheduling those margarita happy hours.

Source:

https://www.birchbox.com/magazine/article/6-scientific-reasons-why-your-friends-really-do-make-you-happier

Ways Your Friends Make You Happier, Healthier and an All-Around Better Person

- Keep you calm.

- Decrease your stress.

- Improve your mood.

- Making new friends can lift your spirits through the release of oxytocin in the body.

Source:

http://www.huffingtonpost.com/2014/07/09/benefits-of-friends_n_5568005.html

4. Health and Fitness

From *The Happiness Report*: On a scale of 1 (low) to 10 (high), please rate your level of agreement for each of the following statements.

- My level of health and fitness is high.

- I work out regularly, eat healthy and sleep an average of 7 – 8 hours a day.

- I purposefully expend and renew the four sources of energy: physical, emotional, mental and spiritual.

Ideas to Boost:

Think about starting small and start even smaller

Five minutes a day, 3x a week.

Source:

http://www.besthealthmag.ca/best-you/mental-health/5-ways-being-healthy-makes-you-happy/6/

More sleep, get outside, eat whole foods, make contact with others, Make exercise a priority. Drink water

Exercise releases feel-good brain chemicals. Reduces anxiety and improves mood.

Source:

https://blog.bufferapp.com/why-exercising-makes-us-happier

Build muscle and stamina. "endorphins are released". Endorphins minimize the discomfort of exercise, block the feeling of pain. BDNF (brain-derived neurotrophic factor) released as brain thinks fight or flight when we exercise. We then feel at ease and thinking is clear.

Key to maximize happiness through exercise: don't do more, but focus on when. The first 20 minutes.

Make exercise a "keystone" habit. Charles Duhigg of The Power of Habit.

Source:

https://www.fastcompany.com/3025957/work-smart/what-happens-to-our-brains-when-we-exercise-and-how-it-makes-us-happier

5. Finances

From **_The Happiness Report_**: On a scale of 1 (low) to 10 (high), please rate your level of agreement for each of the following statements.

- I feel little stress about my current financial circumstances.

- My confidence to meet my financial needs in my later years is high.

- In addition to meeting my living expenses, I am able to save regularly and contribute to causes that are important to me.

Ideas to Boost:

A 7-point formula to accumulate wealth, become happier and achieve financial freedom in the years ahead.

1. Begin to think positively about money.

- When you begin thinking positively about money, you will attract opportunities and open up more doors than you ever thought possible.

2. Rewrite Your Major Goals for Financial freedom.

- Set financial goals for yourself Every day, rewrite and review and think of how you could accomplish them. 5 to 10 minutes. The act of write and rewriting, and thinking about them each morning before your start off, will increase your chances of accomplishing them.

3. Plan every day in advance.   The night before.

4. The Principle of Concentration.   Concentrate on the most valuable use of your time. (CB: Vital Functions).

Enable you to determine the one or two things that you should concentrate on more than anything eels. The things you focus the most on and spend the most time doing should be in direct alignment with your financial goals.

5. Invest in yourself. Audio programs in your car.

6. Ask these magic questions. After every meeting and important event. "What did I do right?" "What would I do differently, next time? By asking and considering, you program into you mind a predisposition to be even better the next time out.

7. Be generous to others. Treat everyone like a million-dollar customer.

Money doesn't buy happiness. The truth is:

- Money is essential to happiness

- Material prosperity predicts life satisfaction

- And the more economic status we achieve, the more we'll feel satisfied with our life.

By choosing to focus on money goals that motivate you, while also embedding a positive mindset towards money, towards yourself and life in general, you will help to achieve both increased wealth and happiness.

Source:

http://www.briantracy.com/blog/financial-success/7-point-formula-for-financial-freedom-personal-finance-make-more-money/

10 Commandments of Financial Happiness - Jean Chatzky

It's time to take back our lives. In order to do that, we need to take control of our money. And we need to do it in a way that will allow us not to feel compromised, guilty and second-rate, but good, happy, smart and sound in our choices.

There is a connection between income and happiness - having enough money to retire, have a good time, purchase the things you want and weather a financial hardship makes you feel more secure and happier.

The research you don't have to be millionaire to be happy. A very strong relationship between feeling in control of your finances and feeling happy about your finances -a and happy with your life. Control over your finances plays a bigger role in determining your life's happiness than being in control of your hob, your health, your friendship, your weight. Wroth striving for. Feel in control

1. Get organized;

2. Pay bills as they come in rather than all at once.

3. Keep tabs on your cash.

4. Save at least 5% of your household income.

5. Protect your family w/ 3-6 months of living expenses, life insurance.

6. Minimize credit-card debt

7. Do onto others. Volunteer, donate.

8. Spend sensibly.

9. Work toward your goals.

10. Communicate with your partner

11. Try not to be consumed with a desire for more. Wanting more doesn't breed contentment; it breeds more wanting.

The conclusion is adopting good money-management habits is like earning significantly more. You don't have to jump on all 10 habits at once. People who adopt half of these habits are significantly happier with their finances Income is just a starting point.

Source:

http://money.cnn.com/2003/09/29/pf/chatzky_commandments_0310/

"Money doesn't buy happiness and it doesn't guarantee happiness, but it impacts your happiness in a huge way."

1. Spend your money on experiences, not things. Family reunion.

2. Spend your money to improve health. Cooking class to learn to prepare healthier food and spend less on eating out.

3. Simplify your life and your finances.

4. Change your routine. "Trying something new can pay off in the long run because you've opened yourself to new experiences that can enrich your life and perhaps even enhance your career in an unexpected way." A day trip or new volunteer activity can bring emotional and financial benefits.

5. Be generous. Can bring great happiness.

6. Pay attention to your life, your friends, your money.

Source:

http://money.cnn.com/2003/09/29/pf/chatzky_comman dments_0310/

6. Spiritual

From *The Happiness Report*: On a scale of 1 (low) to 10 (high), please rate your level of agreement for each of the following statements.

- In my life, I serve a purpose bigger than my own self-interest.

- I've explicitly defined 3-5 core values that describe what I stand for and how I behave.

- I fuel my spiritual energy through frequent reflection, meditation or prayer.

Ideas to Boost:

The question Oprah always asks, "What is your spiritual practice?" What do you do to ground yourself every day?

What do you do to ground yourself, to find that center, to feel balanced? So, that you can go through the day guided by tremendous love and power, the source of which comes from nowhere but within you? Your spiritual practice is whatever routine that helps you shut out the outside world to dwell on the inner world.

You are more powerful, more beautiful, more magnificent than your mind has the capacity to imagine, and this is not to boost the ego which then sets off to abuse these gifts for its own end goal. You are all this with the responsibility to use these assets you've been endowed with for the higher good.

How deep are your roots? Like a 3000-year-old oak tree? The tree withstands windstorms, hurricanes and massive downpours. The tree withstands it all because it is deeply rooted in the ground. IT knows where it belongs and it has no intention of letting anything steal his gifts. IT stands tall and yet remembers its roots.

To be a deeply rooted oak tree, you must learn how to ground yourself. Know that the power resides inside of you, in your core, in your very center, you have an abundance of peace, faith, love, joy resilience, determination, desire and power to do anything - anything at all.

When developing your own spiritual practice, start with these 3 questions:

1. When I feel completely at peace with my life, what am I doing?

2. When I feel out of sorts, what calms me down and makes it right again?

3. Where is my sacred "happy place"? Describe it.

Source:

http://hellogiggles.com/top-5-spiritual-happiness-essentials/

Express gratitude. Show compassion. Show empathy. Ask for guidance. Meditate. Use sound. Listen to your body. Do what you love. Fast. Forgive. Be patient. Tell others the positive stuff. Be vulnerable. Journal. Connect with the World. Read. Be in the Moment. Walk. Breathe.

Source:

http://truththeory.com/2015/10/26/33-simple-ways-to-be-happy-healthy-and-spirituality-connected/

7. Career

From *The Happiness Report*: On a scale of 1 (low) to 10 (high), please rate your level of agreement for each of the following statements.

- I'm fully engaged in my work.

- My career is rewarding in all ways and thriving.

- In addition to the financial benefits work gives me a sense of purpose and accomplishment.

Ideas to Boost:

Mindfulness. More than 80% of the 200-plus people interviewed (Tim Ferris Tools of Titans) have some type of mindfulness practice, typically done on the morning, that helps prepare you to be more self-aware of your thoughts and less emotionally reactive during the day.

Plan your day the night before. Happy mornings start the evening before. Build in something to look forward to, during the day.

Chuck Bolton

Most self-control in the morning. Best time to do something you would rather not do.

Send a thank you email to someone. Makes them happy. Makes you happy, too.

Source:

http://www.forbes.com/sites/kathycaprino/2013/08/26/7-essentials-for-a-happy-and-fulfilling-career/#7f0c0e4d4718

7 Must Haves.

1. Strong boundaries. "Am I living someone else's definition of life and success, or my own?"

2. A Healthy money relationship. "What would I be doing if I were absolutely indifferent to money?"

3. Focus on cultivating happiness. Achor - Success does not breed happiness - it's the other way around.

4. Courage to move away from what's draining you;

5. Gratitude and a vision of what you love;

6. Willingness to get in the cage with your fears.

7. A support circle that empowers you.

Source:

https://www.monster.com/career-advice/article/ten-tips-for-staying-happy-at-work

8. Fun

From **The Happiness Report**: On a scale of 1 (low) to 10 (high), please rate your level of agreement for each of the following statements.

- I pursue hobbies and interests that give me enjoyment and energy.

- I make it a priority to schedule fun activities and events into my calendar on a regular basis.

- I'm highly resilient and able to quickly bounce back from life's ups and downs.

Ideas to Boost:

Probably working too much. Less effective. Don't get the battery re-charged. Creates a bad climate of grind. Pacesetting. Not a good role model.

Pick an evening a week to do something fun. Schedule it. Games, movie, new experience. Something new. Cooking class.

Get a season ticket with others. Forces you to go. Or, check StubHub for something spontaneous.

Ask your partner to schedule on occasion. Better to take turns. Something they like to do. Both have ownership.

More Ideas to Raise Happiness:

- Remind yourself of how good you are. Look at your resume or LinkedIn profile. Make a note of the accomplishments you are most proud of. Your resume is written to make you sound impressive to others - let it have the same effect on you.

- Who do you admire? A hero? Ask when you are stuck, "What would they do if they were here?"

- Use your subconscious. Thomas Edison: "Never go to sleep without a request to your subconscious."

15 Habits That Are Costing You Happiness

1. Comparing Yourself to Others. Comparison has been called the thief of joy and for good reasons. Every minute you spend wishing you were someone else is a minute of your own life wasted. It misses the point of your life - to be you, a once-in-humankind blend of gifts, passions and quirks. Stop looking at others and focus on being you and blossoming into YOUR best self.

2. Trying to give to others without giving to yourself. Buddha, "You as much as anyone in the entire universe deserve your love and affection."

3. Focusing on lack instead of abundance. Switch your lens from lack to abundance and notice the magic surrounding you - fresh air to breather, food to eat, clothing to wear, the beauty of nature, and the endless opportunities for connection, creativity and love. See the miracle of life.

4. Wait for the day when you finally arrive.

5. Numbing your emotions - Have compassion for self.

6. Letting the World define what success means to you.

7. Living in the opinion of others - Eleanor Roosevelt, "No one can make you feel inferior without your consent."

8. Excessive thinking and worrying about the future.

9. Being busy with the wrong things. Henry David Thoreau "It is not enough to be busy. So are the ants." The question: What are we busy about?

10. Putting up with things that don't serve you. Relationships, job, habit.

11. Rehashing the same old thoughts instead of choosing new ones. You are not your thoughts - and you can choose to not take everything they say as the truth. You can also choose to replace or reframe negative thoughts with positive alternatives. Your mind is like a garden - if you take the time to plant seeds in the form of uplifting and empowering thoughts and beliefs, they will flourish into a beautiful worldview that will serve you for the rest of your life.

12. Judging Yourself instead of accepting and loving yourself.

13. Holding grudges form the past. The truth is the past doesn't' really exist - it is a collection of thoughts and images in the mind, which are probably somewhat distorted because whenever we remember something our brain changes the memory slightly. When we forgive the past, we stop carrying ancient pain and fear into the present. We can see the miracle of today and the opportunities it brings clearly again.

14. Complaining about life instead of taking responsibility. IF you want a better life for yourself, be solutions-focused and pour your energy into crating the new instead of wasting your energy fighting the old.

15. Forgetting the bigger picture. Easy to sweat the small things. Remember the bigger picture and purpose of life - love, enjoyment, growth, appreciation, connection, creativity - they lose all significance and you can get back to happiness.

The Two Words that Will Lead to Your Success and Happiness

- The word "Yes' leads to happiness

- The word "No" leads to success.

- "Yes" creates opportunities. Makes more things happen.

- Lots of little good things are the path to happiness.

- Say "Yes" to things and stay active - especially socializing, which makes us happier than almost anything else.

- "No" creates focus.

- The difference between successful people and very successful people is that very successful people say "no" to almost everything.

- Those at the top of their field work obsessively and relentlessly.

- Starts with "protected time" for your important work

- Make a few of your prime hours inviolate. Anything threatening them gets a "no." Period.

Source:

http://theweek.com/articles/450714/two-words-that-lead-success-happiness

7 Ways You're Thwarting Your Own Happiness -

Raj Raghunathan, Author of "If You are So Smart, Why Aren't You Happy?"

"If happiness is important to you, you need to give it priority."

You would think the smarter and more successful you are the happier you would be, right? Wrong!

Life circumstances contribute to only about 10% of happiness.

Happiness Sins. The smart and successful commit some of the very sins that the not-so-smart-or-successful do. The smarter and more successful you are, the greater the chance that you commit these sins.

1. Devaluing happiness: Not giving happiness much priority. Aladdin example. 3 wishes. Only 6% ask for happiness.

2. Chasing Superiority. Translates to wanting to be better than others at something. Results in social comparisons, the tendency to judge oneself relative to others, typically on wealth, power, attractiveness and fame. This tendency is one of the biggest happiness killers.

3. Center of attention. The desperation for love and adulation. Leads to neediness or to avoidance in relationships.

4. Control others and/or outcomes. Being overly controlling is guaranteed to lower happiness.

Other sins include distrusting others, having an indifferent pursuit of happiness and mind addiction - ignoring or underestimating the important of gut instincts and feelings.

Clearly if happiness is important to you, you need to give it priority. Figure out the answer to two important questions: 1. What does happiness mean to me? What activities make me happy? Giving happiness a higher priority should improve your happiness level.

A few things to consider:

1. Maintain a gratitude journal.

2. Random acts of kindness.

3. Gain "internal control." Healthier lifestyle: eat right, move more and sleep better.

Source:

http://time.com/4305128/overcome-deadly-sins-of-happiness/

Appendix 3: Motivating and Inspiring Happiness Quotes

"Find out where joy resides, and give it a voice far beyond singing. For to miss the joy is to miss all." Robert Louis S Stevenson

"Growth itself contains the germ of happiness." Pearl S. Buck

"Happiness is there for the taking – and making." Oprah

"Remember this, that very little is needed to make a happy life." Marcus Aurelius

"True happiness is an acceptance of life as it is given to us, with its diminishment, mystery, uncontrollability, and all." Michael Gellert

"Happiness is when what you think, what you say and what you do are in harmony." Gandhi

"Happiness is in your ability to love others." Leo Tolstoy

"That is happiness: to be dissolved into something compete and great." Willa Cather

"The pleasure which we most rarely experience gives us greatest delight." Epictetus

"One of the secrets of a happy life is continuous small treats." Iris Murdoch

"The capacity for uplift is part of what makes us essentially, euphorically human. Jessica Winter

Happiness is the consequence of personal effort. You fight for it, strive for it, insist upon it, and sometimes travel around the world looking for it. You have to participate relentlessly in the manifestation of your own blessings." Elizabeth Gilbert

"True happiness involves the pursuit of worthy goals. Without dreams, without risks, only a trivial semblance of living can be achieved." Dan Buettner

"The moments of happiness we enjoy take us by surprise. It is not that we seize them, but that they seize us." Ashley Montagu

"The only joy in the world is to begin." Cesare Paves

"Happiness is neither virtue nor pleasure, nor this thing nor that, but simply growth." W.B. Yeats

"Happiness, not in another place, but this place … not for another hour, but for this hour." Walt Whitman

"The supreme happiness of life is the conviction that we are loved." Victor Hugo

"Life is to be enjoyed, not simply endured. Pleasure and goodness and joy support the pursuit of survival." Willard Gaylin

"So many conditions of happiness are available; more than enough for you to be happy right now. You don't have to run into the future in order to get more." Thich Nhat Hanh

"To be kind to all, to like many and love a few, to be needed and wanted by those we love, is certainly the nearest we can come to happiness." Mary Stuart

"Happiness is not something ready-made. It comes from your own actions." Dalai Lama.

"Since you get more joy out of giving joy to others, you should put a good deal of thought into the happiness that you are able to give." Eleanor Roosevelt

"Very little is needed to make a happy life; it is all within yourself, in your way of thinking." Marcus Aurelius Antoninus

"I'd rather be happy than right any day." Douglas Adams

"The Foolish man seeks happiness in the distance, the wise grows it under his feet." James Oppenheim

"Most people are about as happy as they make up their minds to be." Abraham Lincoln

"If you want to be happy, set a goal that commands your thoughts, liberates your energy, and inspires your hopes." Andrew Carnegie

"Thousands of candles can be lit from a single candle, and the life of the candle will not be shortened. Happiness never decreases by being shared." Buddha

"True happiness is not attained through self-gratification, but through fidelity to a worthy purpose." Helen Keller

"Far better it is to dare mighty things, to wing glorious triumphs--even though checkered by failure -- than to rank with those poor spirits who neither enjoy much nor suffer much, because they live in a gray twilight that knows not victory nor defeat." Theodore Roosevelt

"Now and then it's good to pause in our pursuit of happiness and just be happy." Unknown

"So we shall let the reader answer this question for himself: who is the happier man, he who has braved the story of life and lived or he who has stayed securely on shore and merely existed?" Hunter S. Thompson

"The happiness of your life depends upon the quality of your thoughts." Marcus Aurelius

"The greater part of our happiness or misery depends upon our dispositions, and not upon our circumstances." Martha Washington

"Letting go gives us freedom, and freedom is the only condition for happiness. If, in our heart, we still cling to anything - anger, anxiety or possessions - we cannot be free." Thich Nhat Hanh

"Action may not always bring happiness, but there is no happiness without action. "William James

"The more you praise and celebrate your life, the more there is in life to celebrate." Unknown

"All I ask is one thing and I'm asking this particularly of young people: please don't be cynical. I hate cynicism, for the record, it's my least favorite quality and it doesn't lead anywhere. Nobody in life gets exactly what they thought they were going to get. But if you work really hard and you're kind, amazing things will happen." Conan O'Brien

"Everyone wants to live on the top of the mountain, but all the happiness and growth occurs while you're climbing it." Andy Rooney

"The secret of happiness is not in doing what one likes, but in liking what one does." J.M. Barrie

"Most people would rather be certain they're miserable, than risk being happy." Robert Anthony

"Do not look for happiness outside yourself. The awakened seek happiness inside." Peter Deunov

"A flower blossoms for its own joy." Oscar Wilde

"If you want to find happiness, find gratitude." Steve Maraboli

Appendix 4: Happiness Reinvention Game Plan

Happiness Reinvention Game Plan

1. The Why
In Twitter-ese (140 characters or so), what's your why?

Consider defining your why using either of the following templates:

I wake up every day inspired

to_____ so that _____

or

I help_____ do _____

even if _____

2. The Vision
Time Magazine names me *Person of the Year.* What is the summary of this article?

3. The Goals

My breakthrough goals are:

Spiritual

Health and Fitness

Family

Significant Other

Career

Finances

Friends

Fun

My catalyst breakthrough goal is:

4. The Resistance

How is resistance most likely to derail my reinvention efforts?

What will I do to overcome resistance and continue my happiness and reinvention efforts?

What must I reinvent? And for whom?

5. My Daily Routine

Schedule your time wisely. 7-8 hours for sleep. Time for exercise, journaling, gratitude and daily reflection. Time to expend and renew the four sources of energy.

My daily schedule and routine is:

6. My One Word for The Year

Use your one word for the year for inspiration, clarity, and concentration.

My one word for this year is:

Notes

1. Jacobson, Greg. *Think Yourself Happy: Five Changes in Thinking that Will Immediately Improve Your Life*

2. Shawn Achor. *The Happiness Advantage: The 7 Principles of Positive Psychology that Fuel Success and Performance at Work*

3. Joseph McClendon III. *Get Happy Now*

4. Dan Baker and Cameron Stauth. *What Happy People Know: How the New Science of Happiness Can Change* Martin E.P. Seligman. *Authentic Happiness: Using the New Positive Psychology to Realize Your Potential for Lasting Fulfillment Your Life for the Better*

5. Sustainable Development Solutions Network. *World Happiness Report 2016*

6. Chuck Bolton. *The State of Our Happiness in 2017: What We've Discovered*

7. Sonja Lyubomirsky. *The How of Happiness: A Scientific Approach to Getting The Life You Want*

8. Martin E.P. Seligman. *Authentic Happiness: Using the New Positive Psychology to Realize Your Potential for Lasting Fulfillment*

9. George Herbert. *Virtue*

http://www.ccel.org/h/herbert/temple/Vertue.html

10. Chuck Bolton. *The Reinvented Leader: Five Critical Steps to Becoming Your Best*

11. Dale Carnegie. *How to Win Friends and Influence People*

12. The Science of Happiness video – An Experiment in Gratitude – SoulPancake

https://www.youtube.com/watch?v=oHv6vTKD6lgh

13. Bill George. *True North Groups: A Powerful Path to Personal and Leadership Development*

14. Jim Fannin. *The 90 Second Rule*

http://tinyurl.com/lzgrzv

15. Bruce Feiler. *The Secret of Happy Families: Improve Your Mornings, Tell Your Family History, Fight Smarter, Go Out and Play, and Much More*

16. Robert Emmons. *Gratitude Works! The Science and Practice of Saying Thanks*

17. David Niven. *The 100 Simple Secrets of Happy People: What Scientists Have Learned and How You Can Use it.*

18. Karen Reivich and Andrew Shatte. *The Resilience Factor: Seven Essential Skills for Overcoming Life's Inevitable Obstacles*

19. Lewis Smedes. *The Art of Forgiving: When you Need to Forgive and Don't Know How*

20. The Science of Happiness video – *Forgive and Forget – The Phone Call* – SoulPancake

https://www.youtube.com/watch?v=EpclyrcMMHs

21. The Science of Happiness video – *Forgive and Forget* – SoulPancake

https://www.youtube.com/watch?v=809_TlZyB_Y

22. Tony Schwartz. *Be Excellent at Anything: The Four Keys to Transform the Way We Work and Live*

23. David Silverstein. *Become an Elite Mental Athlete: Commit to Building Your Brain and Improving Your Mental Game*

24. Jim Collins. *Good to Great: Why Some Companies Make the Leap...And Others Don't*

25. Doug Lemov. *Practice Perfect: 42 Rules for Getting Better at Getting Better*

Bestselling author Chuck Bolton shows CEOs and senior leaders how to reinvent in a disruptive, crazy busy world so they can achieve happiness, success and maximum impact. He's the president of The Bolton Group LLC, an executive development firm headquartered in Minneapolis. He helps his clients reinvent how they lead, become exceptional leaders and achieve remarkable results. He shows top executive teams how to reinvent so they can perform, create great value and win.

Chuck has coached and consulted more than 1,000 executives and assessed over 100 top teams in the US, Canada, Europe and Israel. Several clients are award winners including: a

CEO who is co-winner of the Nobel prize; a SVP who was the Minneapolis-St. Paul Business Journal "Woman of the Year" in commercial real estate and a CEO named the Ernst and Young Entrepreneur of the Year. Client companies range from early stage companies to Fortune 15 global powerhouses including: Abbott, Baxter, Boston Scientific, Cantel Medical, Covidien, CR Bard, Hewlett-Packard, Medtronic, Optum, Quintiles and UnitedHealth.

Chuck created *Top Team Check*, a proprietary assessment tool and roadmap for extraordinary top team performance. He is the bestselling author of *The Reinvented Me: Five steps to Happiness in a Crazy Busy World*, *The Reinvented Leader: Five Critical Steps to Becoming Your Best* and *Leadership Wipeout: The Story of an Executive's Crash and Rescue.*

Chuck was an executive education instructor at the University of Minnesota, Carlson School of Management, where he created the course: *Optimizing Your Unique Executive Brand*. Chuck served on the Council of Regents, School of Graduate and Professional Programs at Saint Mary's University of Minnesota and was Chairman of the Executive Advisory Board to the Graduate School of Business and Technology.

Chuck appears frequently on KARE11 TV in Minneapolis. He is a sought after speaker to Fortune 500 companies, universities and professional associations. Prior to launching his consulting practice in 2000, Chuck held the position of group vice president, Human Resources, Boston Scientific. He held similar roles at Baxter and American Hospital Supply Corporation.

Chuck received an MBA from Keller Graduate School of Management and a BA from Saint Mary's University of Minnesota. He was recognized at Keller with the "40 for 40" award as a distinguished alum. He has received certificates in executive coaching and emotional intelligence from Corporate Coach U, HayGroup, Adaptiv Learning Systems, the Alliance for Strategic Leadership and the Arbinger Institute.

Chuck Bolton
The Bolton Group LLC
222 S. Ninth Street, Suite 1600
Minneapolis, MN USA 55402
1.800.310.9020
1.612.337.9020
theboltongroup.com

Made in the USA
Lexington, KY
17 January 2017